Racism From the Eyes of a Child

Second Edition

Mathew Knowles, MBA, Ph.D.

DEDICATION

To my parents, Mathew and Helen Knowles, for their motivating influence on my life, and my grandparents and great-grandparents, whose lives I am just getting to know through research. For my daughters, Beyoncé and Solange, in hopes that their children and grandchildren will understand their paternal family's impact on an important era in history.

CONTENTS

"It's like you're looking at this quilt and you see something that takes your breath away as far as its beauty and aesthetic qualities. Yet, at the same time, another piece you see as something that is so ugly and out of place, you wonder how can the two be in the same fabric? That's why I call it a contradiction, and I liken it to Dickens's *A Tale of Two Cities*, because depending on how you're looking at it, you still see undeniable beauty. So, when you said, 'Oscar, we need to go back down there together and just take a tour, to walk around and just see our roots,' I remember thinking to myself, *Why haven't I gone back over the years?*"

—Dr. Oscar Underwood, Jr., March 2017

INTRODUCTION

A Memoir of an Era

The mood of the night came in mean like a southern twister. It stormed its way through the walls as my mother (water) and Grandmother Hester (oil) tried to mix. It ran down the half-mile dirt road leading from the house and out to the main highway stretched before my grandparents' land. Even though I was only five years old, I could feel the tension it produced in both of them. It pushed at my mother until she couldn't take anymore. Despite it being almost midnight, she decided to get us away from Hester's mouth. That meant walking those dark roads, with my older brother Jesse and me in tow, some miles to get to the nearest relative's house.

With only the moon for light, we walked along the side of the main highway until the country quiet stirred with commotion. In the far distance, car horns honked through the roar of engines, and lights approached over the hill to go with the noise. My mother's grip on my hand was fierce as she pulled at us saying, "We have to get in the bushes now!" Before I could ask why, the horns got louder as the lights got nearer. In one quick move, we were down in the brush on the side of the road with her lying protectively over me, praying.

Mean was coming, and it was worse than anything Hester could ever cook up; it was a lot of it by the sounds— bad enough to make a little kid and his mama cry. We lay in the dark, down on the ground, which shook from a parade of peace-breakers.

"If anything happens, take your brother, crawl under that barbed wire, and run as fast as you can!" she told Jesse. Then age fourteen, my brother was bigger and faster than I was, but even he was scared as he looked toward the field full of cows.

He knew we'd have to run—possibly without her. But from what? And why? I wondered. A child always wants to know "why" because the satisfaction they get from the answers helps them develop an understanding of the world. Before I could get any satisfaction, the bushes lit up as if they had been set on fire. Only it was a caravan of headlights and hate burning through the leaves. It seemed like a frozen eternity for a kid with no understanding. Overnight, I went from laughing and running across that beautiful land on my grandfather's own three-hundred–acre slice of Marion, Alabama, to hiding down on it, afraid. Any rights we had toward the pursuit of happiness shattered as the cars passed, honking their hatred in the dark.

Finally, when they were gone, we got up and stepped back onto the dark main highway. As we walked, there were small flags littering the road—the kind with small suction cups you could stick on your car. I bent and picked up a few, studying them for my missing answers. Before I could guess at any, my mother slapped them from my hands with a sharp, "No!" I was too young to understand the terror left by that passing KKK caravan, which was either coming from or going to a rally. I was too naive to realize the immediate danger we faced from Klansmen in 1957 or even the very symbol of hate that I held in my hands. I can now appreciate my mother's bravery and whatever courageous moves she would have made if they had spotted us.

When she asked my brother to take me to the pasture and run, underneath her fright, I saw something else but was too young to name the expression. It took getting old enough to join her and my entire generation in fighting discrimination to label that look—even when it sits under a mask of fear. If I had a single hard word for it, I would call it "grit." A polite way to describe it is "determination to survive, even while knowing someone else doesn't want you to." It is courage even when you're scared to death. I had to conjure it many times, as I grew up "the first" in so many instances, like the first to integrate a place I was told I had no business. Such situations affected me deeply.

I saw only one side of racism that summer in Marion, yet from the eyes of a child, it offered a lasting impression of it. The memory of the Klan was flavored by the overall mean-spiritedness of the night, starting with my angry grandmother. It was my first, but not my last, childhood encounter with racial tensions in Alabama. They were frequent and loud during the years I came of age—the 1950s through the early 1970s—particularly the summer of 1963. I still have the cattle prod burn on my arm as a memento.

The mean spirit of racism found me in Marion and later growing up in Gadsden, Alabama. I also caught it in college in Tennessee, then in corporate America, and later in the entertainment industry. It is ingrained in our national fabric. Once you see those lines as a child, you can easily spot them later on, even when they're subtle. Racism is now a trending topic in an era in which we all view the same headlines showing us it is not as dead as we would like it to be. In fact, it openly wears a variety of faces in every color as we head into 2018.

As a historic site for educators, Marion, Alabama, was full of lessons for a child like me. Yet, I learned most from people who managed to walk tall around corn-fed racists. These are men who made me proud and women who taught me to fight back. Studying their lives helped me piece together a quilt not too unlike the one my cousin Oscar Underwood described in a talk with me—one both ugly and beautiful. The differences between the two views are thin on some patches with lines so stark they hurt your eyes.

These ugly parts did discernable damage to many of us —I know it did to me. Yet, they also formed us into fighters and against-odds achievers. This book examines this racial tapestry through research and interviews with others in my family to see if the events we lived through in the South—during America's most openly racist past—helped condition our lives.

Maya Angelou wrote, "I hope to look through my life at life… I want to use what has happened to me—is happening to me—to see what human beings are like." Unlike her, I had moved deliberately through my adult life, hardly giving my childhood in the South any hard glances. Now watching the media broadcasting filled with words we thought were relegated to the past—lynching, marches, protests, white supremacy—I felt I had to look again for my future bloodline's sake. How would they know that their own family fought and, in many cases, won victories against discrimination? Our children should have names and faces tying them to this tremendous social movement

.

By looking back at the parts that I repressed for being too painful, I hope to make sense of these racial contrasts seen throughout my life. Racism, being such a bold statement of hate, looms as something monstrous to an innocent child. It is a poor representation of what being human is all about. The hate children experience in any form can shape the person they become. How they later process it as adults can even shape their families.

This book is only a memoir insofar as it timelines my own coming of age with that of America's through the era of racial segregation and the fight against it. It is also a chance for voices formerly buried in census records, old crumbling marriage certificates, obits, and photos to have a small say. They speak by having lived through conditions few of us would understand today. Some married each other not always for love but rather for its support system, surviving better in groups against oppression and inadvertently breeding more soldiers in the fight. Ancestors of ours faced racial torment so intense, the mean men behind it would dare burn a symbol as sacred as across in the name of hate.

These are bits of my own family, but you will be surprised at how many of you can scratch an elder and find some who faced similar discriminations. You might just find traces of your own family's history in the civil rights movement if you start to ask questions. It's never too late. You may just find throughout those same eras of struggle that your bloodline is among those who left historic marks on the era. If you do trace them, I hope you allow them to echo along with mine to tell this generation the truth of how it was. The voices lost among those old family mementos carved their own places in history. Surviving slavery, Jim Crow, many a Bloody Sunday, and even to this day, they survive through us— because we are here as proof that they made it. Yet, we can be honest about the distance left to go because while there is progress, there are still the glaring contradictions that even a child can see.

I could never mend the country's racial chaos in a book, but I am sure I can fix a chaotic part of myself by writing it. I think that is where everyone needs to start—by searching within your own history of hate, pain, struggle, and the victory over it all—as far back as you can trace. That might just be the key that unlocks the mysteries of what makes us human, making some love and accept and others hate and segregate. This book explores my life through one eye while the other remains wide open on the current times. By the end of the book, I will stare straight into the same mirror I will invite you to look in to question your own journey.

By looking with honesty, you can examine not just racism but all forms of meanness that discriminates and alienates based on any difference, much less color. The world's racial attitudes, good or bad, shape all of us eventually— whether saints or sinners, resisters or racists. If we each at least come clean about what we see in that mirror, we can work to create a more beautiful image for the children yet to come.

PART I

ROOTS IN RACISM

THEY CALLED HIM MISTER HOGUE

Summers for me as a child meant leaving my native Gadsden, Alabama, to go spend time enjoying days having fun all over the three hundred acres of land belonging to my grandparents, Dave and Hester Hogue, down in Marion, Alabama, which was "the country" to most folks. Standing at a statuesque six feet five inches, my grandfather wasn't just called farmer, landowner, and moonshine distributor—all of which he was— they also called him "Mister." Both whites and blacks alike in his community respected him, and I witnessed it firsthand as a child.

One Saturday during a summer visit, two older white men knocked on my grandfather's front door. "Is Mr. Hogue home?" one of them asked. I had never heard a white man call a black man Mister. I looked at my cousin, who was equally as shocked but obviously proud. In fact, we spent the whole day bragging about it. It stands out as the moment when I realized a man could be treated with dignity by anybody—even if he were black.

My grandmother Hester was simply somebody you had to work around if you wanted any fun. Otherwise, that is all I remember having, thanks to my grandfather. He was the first to show me how to ride a horse, shoot rifles, and how to fish those lakes. I proudly watched him, a brilliant entrepreneur, negotiate leasing some of his three hundred acres to the local timber mill, who would, in turn, cut down the trees so that he could farm the next season. Even a kid could see he was smart.

As much as there was deep-seated hatred for men of color (strong enough that even a child could see that too), if you looked hard or in the right places, you could catch a rare breed of respect. After almost meeting the Klan, it gave me a balance and a comparison for how a man could walk through life—even one filled with hatred directed at him—and still get some of them to respect him. I have a clearer memory in my head than I do a photograph of my grandfather. The one I have is only a blurred reflection of someone so bold. He was a man who taught me that by walking tall, you never had to internalize the hatred, and you never had to stoop or cower under it. With your head as high as my granddad's, all you had to do was look it in the eyes.

(Dave Hogue's actual moonshine jug circa 1930s)

"I always thought everybody liked him 'cause he made that corn liquor! They say the best around! I have one of those big old bottles he sold it in. Everything else is gone. The land was sold from what we know to the state for a highway." — **Chiquita Knowles-Ash**

(Hester Hogue. From the Knowles Family Collection)

"We would go down there and visit my grandmamma and grandfather in the summertime. Grandmamma was tall and dark-skinned. I remember she used to have that temper. My mom had it too. It was a lot of tension because of the fact my mom left Marion. My grandmother wanted her to stay and work on the farm, and she didn't want that kind of life for herself, and so I think that was the reason they didn't get along." —**Chiquita Knowles-Ash**

(Left: Hester and Dave Hogue. Right: Helen and Mathew Knowles)

HESTER & HELEN
THE TALE OF TWO MOTHERS

Knowing how much of our lives are shaped by our families, I didn't want to revisit my memories of Marion with just one-dimensional portraits—not of a mean grandmother or a meaner city. I needed to dig deeper into the roots of how it might have affected critical and developmental aspects of us. My perspective is that all the traumatic racial infractions we witnessed or heard about influenced more than we realized growing up.

It occurred to me, while looking at the family pictures and the images from those times, that the environment shaped both my parents' and grandparents' personalities. What I didn't understand about them is equal to how little I knew about the era in which they grew up. They too were influenced by the treatment they received as children because all humans are. This made me look closer at them—particularly my grandmother, Hester Hogue, because she casts such an angry reflection through so many of our childhood accounts. She made such a perfectly humanizing example of what hard life did to a person in an environment that matched in bitterness.

After finding Grandma Hester's marriage certificate and her name on a census when she was a young woman, I looked at her picture again. Her portrait is a snapshot of my family's DNA—like her or not. As with any relative—love them or hate them—blood runs, regardless. I look at her and realize I never knew her. It is understandable that a child sees an adult—whether they were kind or mean—as a one-dimensional person. However, as another adult, you can look at their vulnerabilities and possible struggles and eventually add a few things up.

In looking at my maternal side of the Hogues and Moores, I contacted two of my closest relatives: first cousin Linda Hogue-Anglen and a second cousin, Dr. Oscar Underwood, both connected to me by my grandparents there in Marion. I also took notes from the recall of my younger sister, Chiquita Knowles-Ash (and for my Gadsden years that I cover later, my first cousin on the Knowles's side, Robert Avery). Each carries their own points of view as children growing up or visiting the South. Each walks with a lasting impression of their own youth there.

I started by talking about my grandfather because he was easier—both to describe and in regard to his nature. Yet, his wife, my mother's own mother, was as I described—contrary enough to have made us want to leave her presence in the dead of night. Was she just hateful, or was there a backstory to her meanness? As much could be asked of racism. This is what I wondered as I looked at her portrait—at a piece of my own DNA. When seeing a face that might carry even the smallest trace of your own character, how is that not like looking in a mirror? Looking for a piece of ourselves in the nose, a chin, around the eyes...and what about in temperament?

It opened the floodgate of questions about family, and the door to researching them would have me ask questions about the entire era. If you do a Google search and happen to stumble across her name, you will find little but a census-compiled footnote, starting with her parents and her birth and ending with a reference to my mother.

Pinkney Moore and Arenia (Goree) Moore

↵ **Parents of Hester Moore born 1891 in Alabama. Hester married Davis Hogue Dec 10, 1913, in Perry, Alabama.**
↵ **Parents of Lue Helen Hogue-Knowles (my mother).**

She died July 4th, 1965, in Gadsden, Etowah, Alabama (in my family's home there) and when she did, she left as a one-dimensional character to all of us kids. This census footnote tells us nothing, especially after seeing the names of her father and grandfather for the first time and tracing them back to years extending into the era of slavery. I could imagine long lines of cousins walking around that we know nothing about—every damn where.

Hester's father, Pinkney Moore, didn't die until May 12, 1944, in Perry County. That means he was around for my mother and older brother to have known, passing away only eight or nine years before I was born. Yet, I had no stories handed down about this man born in 1853. Without their testimonies in our ears, what do we know of the hardships they came from? Who was my great-great-grandfather, Calvin Moore, born in 1824?

Keep in mind the dates <u>September 22, 1862, to January 1, 1863,</u> which cover the Emancipation Proclamation. You can see some of the names I mentioned were born *before* that, and some lived on during the entire post- slavery Reconstruction era. That does not necessarily make them slaves in Alabama, as many freedmen existed all over, but it raises a possibility some could have been. They could have been Native Americans too, as family legend often has it in the South for both black and white people. Later, I would find out they had good reason to be.

Our parents and grandparents told us few stories of the old folks because not many, during childhood, even asked about them. If we did, replies were short on details because time was not often wasted on small talk with kids. Also, who back then wanted to reminisce on days when their family was in or just coming out of chains? Fewer still had stories of where they came from *before* the chains. Not many details are found in the records of former slaves, even into the late 1800s. Listed as "born in parts unknown" (at least to us), could those parts have been Africa or the Caribbean? Or were they Native American roots? Racism uses, at its primary base, an eraser to rub out histories and facts and therefore true knowledge, which we all know has power. It strips that away as simply as neglecting to record if your people were once African warriors or Native braves.

Sure, a well-paid genealogist could uncover a good deal of the mystery for us, but it still begs the questions: Why are so many of us disconnected from our past in the first place? Is it worsened by the absence of conversations between generations? Do we lack pride in what used to be? It is understood that slaveholders deliberately broke the line of history since it didn't serve them. Once black families came together after emancipation, how many still held their tongues about who we once were out of shame or lack of knowledge?

What a burden to mysteriously arrive in a segregated South by birth surrounded by large portions of the population that appear to hate you and remain ignorant of your heritage and your people because your parents are forced to raise you without it. Bottom line—there are few personal details about ancestors in some black families, and mine was one.

I wonder—if we had known how they survived that environment, would it have made a stronger impact on those of us raised in silence? Did anything push its way through the bloodlines we need to know about? There are certainly signs that the defiance to survive did, but what about medical or emotional traits? To know early dementia, heart issues, or diabetes run that far back might go a long way toward helping us break generational handicaps.

My family became more mysterious on paper as I sifted their lives through records found. I regret that I didn't ask these questions as a child. When we left pursuing a better life than what our folks had, we also walked away from who they were and who their folks were. We can't grow up with any sense of pride in what our ancestors owned or accomplished if we don't know about it. We also can't understand what made them the type of people they were. My grandfather was renowned for his shrewdness and kindness just as his wife Hester is sadly remembered mostly for her temper. It influenced me subtly by being such the contrast to my sweet-tempered grandfather and showing me how two seemingly opposing forces could live together under one roof for so long.

It was a foreshadowing of what my cousin Oscar refers to as the tale of two cities. It was the beauty I found after learning how to love the land from my grandfather; it was the ugly feeling forced off it by Hester and into the kind of hate that can kill you. To dismiss what set up those conditions would be to miss some necessary juncture I was supposed to take to the past. Since I knew nothing about where my folks were originally from or even how Granddad got that land, I started asking questions of cousins descended from the Hogues and the Moores and all their extensions. I needed a clearer picture of Marion and not just my own.

I also wanted to keep their voices in the retelling of their own childhoods there. Sometimes your family's recollections won't match—that's when you know it's the whole picture. Through their childish eyes, they took their own snapshots of the era. They sealed them in their mental memory books in their own ways, just like I did mine. That's what makes it a quilt—the beauty and honesty of different but interconnected pieces. We need to see where the lessons were hidden in those memories so we don't walk away with just old pictures. What did they also view as children, which made at least three of us never want to go back to the South? What all were we running from, and what did everyone leave behind on those three hundred acres the family eventually lost?

FROM THE EYES OF LINDA HOGUE-ANGLEN

"When I was twelve, I was allowed to take a train and go down by myself to Marion. I stayed six weeks, and I hated it. I can say that my grandfather was just wonderful. He was a dynamic, down to earth, kind, and loving man who took out time to be with his grandchildren. With my grandmother…I just saw a stern matriarch. Maybe that's just the way she was —hard. As a child looking at their grandparents, all I can say was that she was in charge of everything, but she was a very strict woman. That really stuck with me as to my attitude toward one grandparent versus the other.

"For example, a memory that stands out is when we went to town. Once, when my grandmother did her shopping and my grandfather was socializing, I had to sit in the funeral home (at the foot of a casket). I had never been around anything like that. When my grandfather collected me, he complimented me for being so patient, and I asked him for an ice-cream cone. He was like, 'Oh yeah, we can go get you one.' It immediately made me happy until my grandmother came back and said, 'Naw, that child don't need that!' That's an example of how he would give us so much love, and she would seem as though she was snatching it away.

"My family would travel from Ohio to Perry County in Marion, Alabama, probably every summer. My brother was three years older and my sister two years younger. As kids, we would join all my young cousins and have a lot of fun whenever we went down, especially when the family from Gadsden would come over, like Aunt Helen with Jesse and Mathew. It seems like my grandfather would just always make it worth our while to be there, but my grandmother…we just tried to stay out of her way. We used to have big family reunions. They would have the Tuckers and the Hogues and some other family like the Moores, who were extremely close to us, such as my grandmother Hester's twin brothers Sydney and Gydney Moore.

"Uncle Syd's wife was named Marie, and it was to their house we would walk to visit. It was less than five miles from my grandparents' house to theirs. That was the only other walking-distance family there. I was just a little one, but I remember so much of how Granddad was so wonderful and thoughtful, and my grandmother was not…. And then I thought it was just my attitude until I talked to some of my other cousins, the children of my dad's brothers and sisters. They said the same thing. That that's just the way she was. Probably, looking at it from an adult view now, life was hard there. I look at the way the house they lived in was made. I know people often built their own houses then, especially on farmland, but it seemed old and uncomfortable by the time I was a child visiting. It only had one little plot of flowers to the right of the house—purple flowers that would open up at a certain time of day and then close back. That was the only pretty thing about that house I remember….

(Example of rural house during the Hogues' era. Home of Bud Fields —Alabama sharecropper. Hale County, Alabama, 1935, by Walker Evans)

(Hester Hogue's actual butter churn circa 1950s)

"The house was wood with an old tin roof that sat quite a distance from the road, so you had to drive maybe half a mile to get to the front yard. When you walked up two or three steps, it had a flat porch, and on it was that butter churn of hers. That was what my grandmother had me work the milk in, up and down with a stick, to make the cream and butter. I remember being out there and getting tired; I was a city kid, and I wasn't used to that. But I had to keep on doing that until she told me I could stop. She was just a hard taskmaster.

"Then when you went into the house, to the left side of it was the 'front room,' they would call it. There, and in some bedrooms, you could look through and see down to the ground because the house was lifted up. You could see the chickens walking and clucking under there and everything else with them. A big aluminum tub was in an alcove area below a large window, and more than one person would take a bath in it. Then they threw the water out that window.

"Outside was a hen house and an outhouse. Coming from Cleveland, you can imagine what the rural South was like for me. But when you think about the people who lived there, it was what they had and were used to, so maybe it didn't bother them. For me at age twelve, it was not a very pleasant setting. It was a hard life. When you think about other things going on in the community between whites and blacks, it must have been a lot to bear. But she had to keep it together because it was her family."

***

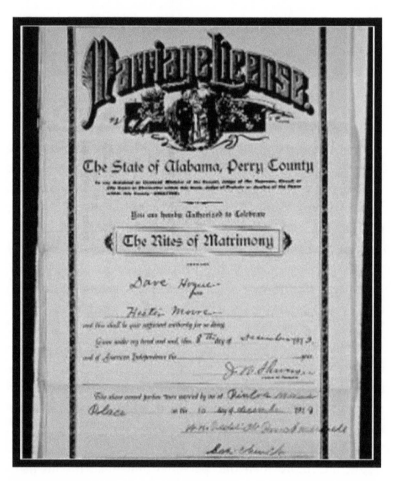

Once I had spoken to my cousin Linda, I wondered more about my grandparents' relationship under the conditions of that

 In 1910, Dave Hogue was 26 years old and head of his household. With him lived his mother, Rosetta, who was 68 years old and a widow. Also living with him was a brother, Robert, who was 17, a nephew, Leander, who was 14, a nephew, John Hill, who was 15 a niece, Mary Rose, who was 18 and another niece who was Rosetta and 12 years old. He was not married during this time

rough life, especially after finding their marriage license and seeing the signatures where Dave and Hester agreed to marry and start our bloodline. This was when the flood of questions began, and it opened up more about my culture and heritage also. This led to the exploration of who I had become as a man and what traits I had inherited from them, if any.

The mystery of it all sat in those mementos, including Hester's butter churn, which my sister still has. Were they in love back in 1913 when she was twenty-two years old (born 1891) and he was forty-two years old (born in 1871) and already head of a household? Was it a May-December romance or one of convenience? My grandfather had his widowed mother living with him when he was twenty-six years old and was listed as the head of household in the census. He lived with what looks like ten other people to feed. Maybe marriage just wasn't a priority for him at that time.

Had either one of them had relationships before? It seems back then that even twenty-two was old when it came to an age when folks got married. At age forty-two, I wonder if Granddad had waited that long to marry. I had zero memory of them as a couple, but I wondered if Linda, who was older, could remember any details about them.

Linda—

"He was never mean around her that I observed. He never said anything or did anything around us to show he was mean to her. But I never saw them being close to one another or him giving her a hug either. Never saw him touching her fondly or giving her a kiss. He was never that way in front of us, at least. So I don't know what was going on. Now Uncle

Sydney, who lived nearby...he and Aunt Marie had a wonderful relationship. She was a loving, caring person, and the whole house was one full of fun and love. Lots of cheerfulness. I never saw them openly affectionate either, but even as a child, you could just tell the difference between the two households. They may not have had as much land as Granddad, but they seemed to be living a little better.

"Maybe it was just the household and because of how welcoming Aunt Marie was. Even when they later came to Cleveland, we stayed close to that side of the family. As a child, I may not have remembered their house as detailed as I did my grandparents', but I knew that it was a good place whenever we were there."

* * *

In the thirteenth census in 1910, Davis Hogue is listed as the head of household with his mother, Rosetta, widowed and living with him. By the Census of 1940, carried out in Election Precinct One in Perry, he is age sixty-one and a married head of household. The prior residence is listed as "same house." Was it the same land he eventually bought up, or did he inherit it from one of his parents Jim and/or Rosetta? We all wondered when the ownership of three hundred acres (and was that the precise number?) by a black man in the segregated South in the 1940s and '50s entered the picture.

Did they give exact information, or did the census-takers inaccurately list dates and ages? That same census lists Hester

Hogue and my own mother, spelled "Lu Helen Hogue," at age eighteen. Hester would have been thirty-three years old when my mother was born by this account. I noticed it says "renting" on the census, yet by the time I was running and riding across all those acres, he owned all three hundred acres of it, and everybody in town talked about it. Only now do questions arise to which we have no answers, and none of them are left living to help. Maybe they held back details from us as children because there was little positive information to report about "the old days," or they simply followed the "kids stay out of grown folks' business" rule so that we stopped asking. As a result, whole generations of information have slipped away.

The obituaries tell only pieces of their story if anybody bothers to keep them around, but they are useful. They are mini bios on whatever significant contributions they made in this world but still a sad and too-brief summary of a relative you love. If I could find my grandparents' obituaries, would they tell of how they got their land and built houses with their hands on it—or how they lost it? I had to start somewhere, so I again asked my cousin Linda for her recollections.

—Linda

"I don't know how he got it; no one ever talked about it. But I know there was a lot of confusion about it among the brothers and sisters when it was lost because they were saying that instead of working together to keep the land and sell the lumber that was on it, they wanted to divide it up. And in that division was a lot of confusion, and they probably lost a lot of what they had. I do believe that there was a court battle from bits and pieces I heard about later—mostly them saying how they lost it because the brothers and sisters were not all together and how they could've kept it."

***

What my mother, Helen Hogue-Knowles, explained to me was a bit more detailed than what Linda heard. Somewhere over the years, my mother and grandfather purchased twenty-five acres of that land together. They partnered together to make that last buy; however, when my granddad died, that portion became a part of the dispute. The four children were to divide all of the land equally—that was clear. However, since my mother and grandfather had a deal that split twenty-five additional acres, her twelve and a half acres couldn't then be divided with her siblings. That is where the confusion came in. Either she couldn't prove it, or there was a mix-up with the deeds; the outcome was the disagreement. This ultimately led to the dissolution of ownership of all the land, although how it played out, the details have been mostly lost. I did wonder why the younger members of our Marion family had left the land in the first place.

—Linda

"I haven't been to Marion for years. Young people knew that they could get better jobs if they came up north. My dad, Robert Louis Hogue, went north to work at age eighteen. He and my mom married early, and then he brought her to Cleveland, Ohio, where the three children in my family were born and raised. I know my dad came up and started working the steel mills where he was for years. He could make better money and support his family better by leaving."

***

This was the case with many families once the steel mills and other plants opened to the north. Housing would have seemed better and opportunities brighter than under the shadows of slavery still lingering in some white folks' eyes. Even race relations were better for those migrating families, as Linda told me. However, for those born, raised, and who would eventually pass away in "the country," the land and all its mysteries were all they had. Still, I couldn't shake that memory of those white men at the door calling my granddad "Mister." It seems like such an insignificant thing, but when looked at from a child's perspective, what you're hoping to find is a hero in a time of so much open hate—hatred that was hard enough to make you leave even your heroes behind for a better life.

In the end, adding up all the stories from my cousins about why we ended up leaving or not going back, it was because of that not-so-subtle hate—economic and emotional. Once we did leave, the level of discrimination, segregation, and out-there racism dropped to almost zero for at least one of us—Linda. While aware of the violence and protests of the '50s and '60s, she and her siblings were mostly kept from it.

As she recounts:

—Linda
"I felt wonderful growing up in Cleveland. We had a pleasant, comfortable life because my dad was a hard worker. He worked in a steel mill, but he would also do landscaping. While he was out being such a good breadwinner, Mom was able to stay home with us. She said he never had time to count his money; he would just put it on the table, and she would handle all the household finances. He worked all the time, but I do remember him going to church with us every Sunday. A family life like that made childhood special. We had relatives who had moved to the house in the front of us, so we would have a lot of family affairs together. We were never very segregated in our area, and the feeling you had in Marion of always watching out for something negative to happen was never there.

"When we got ready to go into high school, we moved to a predominantly white neighborhood and a nice public school. I graduated from high school in the '60s, and even though a lot was happening in the country, there wasn't anybody that I personally knew who was involved. There may have been incidents of racism in our community, but we didn't hear about it, or if we heard about it, they weren't personally involved. We simply didn't have any problems. No one bothered us. Keep in mind, my mother kept us close; we were homebodies. Growing up home in Ohio, I didn't encounter any of those things that Mom used to say she experienced when they went south.

"Like when they went down, they weren't allowed to stay in hotels, so they would have to pull over off the road so my dad could rest. There were black people's water fountains and then white people's ones. I remember one time, my brother went to the wrong restroom. He was too young to read, so he went into the one for whites only. Nobody bothered him or said anything, but Mama was nervous. Later, when the Birmingham riots happened, we had a close cousin who used to come up and often visit with his family; he was involved in the marches and riots. I just remember us being very worried about him. But none of us in my community ever were involved.

"I now live in the South, in Atlanta, and I have to say, all of the fears you might have about the South, based on all those things we heard about growing up...I have been here three years and have never had one problem. Even white people here hug me and treat me almost like family, and I have to say, I was pleasantly surprised. That whole southern hospitality thing is real for me, and I wasn't expecting it. I suppose all my life, God has put me in a safe zone, and I've just been blessed, and I'm grateful."

***

Like Linda's parents, when our folks left the farm, it seems their goal was to create a prettier picture for their kids—something better than the time-faded, tin-roof shacks and the heated bigotry they baked under, not to mention the need to break free of their parents' control like all youth eventually want to do. Those like my cousins up north got to grow up the way kids dream of, with an intact family, middle-class communities, good schools, and fun. Knowing what those of us who remained in the South dealt with, I could appreciate the differences in our environments.

There was one thing still bothering me about the couple that my grandparents were because it was such a contrast and part of my grandmother's temperament is what drove so many away. I had a few more questions for Linda. If our grandfather, Dave Hogue, was known as a well- respected man that so many people loved, how did he manage to live so long with Hester, who seemed his opposite? This made me examine whether a twenty-year gap and a hate-filled South between them left a cold spot for Hester beneath Dave's wing. His level of respect by the local townspeople—did it extend to her also?

—Linda

"…I don't think she got any of that, and that may have been the problem. As an adult and a woman, looking back, it makes sense. As a child, I didn't understand that, but looking back, I do."

***

We could both only speculate on my grandmother's possible hard life. Everyone agrees she worked hard in the fields and keeping the house. Did she do it with very little affection or acknowledgment as a wife? Was living under the adoring light of my grandfather, while she did all the housework, what made Hester so mean? Perhaps she had greater depth to her personality that living and working in the hard South (even on your own land) held back. If she had her own dreams, longings, and attributes, we never got to know them. My sister Chiquita, although nine years younger than I, had her own childhood recollections, including being there in the house with Dave and Hester in their final days.

—Chiquita

"Even though they didn't get along, they were a lot alike, my mother and grandmother. I know my grandmother was the one that taught my mother how to sew and how to make her own butter. I still have the churn that she used. Grandmamma took sick, and eventually both of my grandparents had to move in with us. I think Granddad really loved my grandmother from what I saw. It's a different love when you get older and sick. She ended up dying before he did after being sick a long time. I know he loved her because of how he took care of her once she got what they call 'sundowners' and stayed bedridden most of the time. He was tender with her, and that's how people showed love.

"You can't look at it like we do now. Like when I was little, I had to create love inside myself because my mother wasn't the kind that just gave it out like that and neither was her mother. They showed it in the food they cooked, the roof over your head. I can remember life seeming real hard for them, and they were just fighters because of that fact. Both of them were real fighters and fearless; I don't remember them backing down or acting afraid of nothing or nobody.

"Like at the house in Marion, one time when we were kids visiting, a snake dropped down from the loft up where me and Mathew slept. My grandmother had made these big ole biscuits that we would eat with sorghum syrup because that was everybody's staple in the country for breakfast. When that six-foot snake dropped down, us kids started hollering and screaming until Grandmamma came running with those super-size biscuits and started throwing them at the snake to get it away from us. Then she got a stick, picked it up, and threw it outside. I'm telling you, she was fearless.

"When she got sick and they came to live with us, I wasn't in school yet. Mama used to leave me there, and that's when I could see Grandmamma Hester was different. Weaker. Mama would leave me there for my granddaddy to watch while she worked. She would have already cooked the food, and it would be in the oven for him to heat up to feed me lunch. One day, he went to the oven to get the food and fell down. I ran to a neighbor's house and told them he was sick, and they got there and found him dead."

***

My sister reminding me of that big snake and how Hester saved us from it is why this quilt needed many different pieces of memory to be whole. One picture from one child fills in the space where another one drops off. It's easy to get older and forget the lines that draw it all together. My sister and my cousins had their own images of youth, and together the family tapestry— the beauty and the ugly—was honestly forming for me. I saw from the pieces that these grandparents of ours had love lives (or loveless lives), dreams and desires, fears and fights of their own.

We got their personalities in raw form. No therapist waited after emancipation with some post-traumatic stress treatments for any of them. Neither did the slave owners get therapy. Did they need some for their cruel and vicious practices? How many came from folks who had been traumatized for their beliefs? How many had ancestors who were beaten, tarred and feathered, chained in dungeons, raped, and torn on racks...all because of their differences? Is that trauma what some white immigrants' descendants subconsciously inherited and passed on to their children? Is evidence being found in their mean actions against the Native American, African, and Caribbean people they enslaved? Perhaps there was a trickle down of mistreatment, and not one of them got the kind of help we seek today after such trauma.

Was there internalized bitterness in the slaveholder families—from what drove them away from Europe and other ports to the wars and all those battles with the Natives, Spanish, etc. in between? Did the founders pass on the effects of such stress? Was it a case of "hurt people hurt people" or just plain evil?

I was getting somewhere with my family picture but needed to understand their environment better. Looking at the underbelly of Marion's ugly side, it ran opposite to their efforts to put so many notable achievers on the map. My cousin Oscar was able to explain the city's academic and racial backstory and added a significant point of view from his youth. It was he who first pointed out the quilt analogy that literally wove together what we saw as a whole.

FROM THE EYES OF
DR. OSCAR UNDERWOOD, JR.

"You know as I prepared to talk with you, I realized that I had not spent a lot of time thinking about why I had pursued the things I had in life. Nor did I understand why the Knowles family had achieved such wonderful things. Yet, I heard my mother and my grandmother in my ear as I reflected on the various people who had their roots, and still do, in that small hamlet. Here I was born in Marion, Alabama; even though I left there at three years old and was raised in Ft. Wayne, Indiana, my roots are there. As a kid, I was about thirteen years old when I first became aware of Dr. Martin Luther King. I remember at one point we were watching TV, and it showed Mrs. Coretta Scott King. My mama said to me, 'You see her? That lady there is Dr. King's wife, and when we were kids, we went to the same school. She was such a nice girl. I remember that at recess, she would let me braid her hair.'

"Even though she hadn't seen her for years, her connection to my mother was significant to me at that age. I later realized that Coretta Scott King was the valedictorian of this historical school there in Marion—Lincoln Normal School —attended not only by her but also Ambassador Andrew Young's wife, Jean Childs Young, whose mom was also one of the teachers there at the time. I now reflect on others I have since heard about who were also connected, such as Bishop T.D. Jakes's mom, who graduated from Lincoln Normal. In fact, the city was native soil to many great achievers, like Albert Turner, who was the field secretary for the Southern Christian Leadership Conference (SCLC) and Dr. King's point man in Marion on the voting rights initiative. (An article at the time of his death speaks of his role in the civil rights movement and adds details on how he led the voting rights march. History shows this was that fateful Selma-to-Montgomery movement that started on March 7, 1965. It forever linked the Edmund Pettus Bridge, which once flowed innocently over the Alabama River, to one Bloody Sunday.)

"Albert Turner, the Scott-King, and the Young families —in all these there is a heavy emphasis on education with them. Marion, for such a small place, is known to have produced a large number of African Americans who went on to get advanced degrees. There is a rich academic foundation there as a result. Alabama State University started in Marion as part of Lincoln Normal High School. A missionary society ran it at the time and realized they needed a teacher-training component, and so they added Lincoln Teachers' College. When the two separated, and the high school and college divided, they then moved the teachers' college component to Montgomery and became Alabama State University.

"I see it as a paradox and a contradiction both beautiful and yet ugly. It's beautiful when you look at its genuine commitment from about 1867, immediately after the Civil War had ended, up for about 100-plus years, in protecting the human dignity of African Americans in its populace—as far as education was concerned. These were primarily people who were not African American for the most part, who served as the driving force to make sure that education was a priority there. It was striking to me.

"In my research, I found not only is there education at its roots but also entrepreneurship. Mrs. King's father, Mr. Obadiah Scott, was a businessman who owned a store there about nine miles outside of town. People in that area could get food and other things that they needed and avoid coming all the way into town. He was well loved in Marion and that whole surrounding area as a result. Mathew's grandfather, Dave Hogue, was a businessman and landowner also, like a lot of our cousins. One was among the few African American cab drivers to have their own cab company.

"I think what we would find there is how many African

Americans used their access to education, but also all those who did not have any but still used their skills to make sure they were able to take care of their families. Even though there was extreme poverty, they were put in a place where they had to do something to survive. We have learned that those moments are some of the most precious ones because at that time we discover strength and abilities that were inherent in us that do not surface until there is a demand put on them. They achieved their abilities despite the tenor of that time. Greatness came from Marion with an entrepreneurial and academic spirit.

"We could say that it is happenstance when you look at Bishop Jakes's family or the Knowles family or before us what Mrs. King and Mrs. Young went on to do. Looking at what I'm doing as far as my own college and my own prep school and the ministry as well now…I don't think it's happenstance at all. There are probably thousands of others we don't know about. I believe that our ancestors somehow passed on to us that entrepreneurial spirit. That is the beautiful part of Marion —its historical commitment to education, but then there's another part. When you look at history immediately after the Civil War and from that point forward, it seems as if Marion, and that surrounding area, is best likened to what Dickens would call *A Tale of Two Cities*.

"It's like you're looking at this quilt, and you see something that takes your breath away as far as its beauty and aesthetic qualities. Yet, at the same time, another piece you see as something that is so ugly and out of place, you wonder how can the two be in the same fabric. But it is. Because when you look at the ugliness, we're looking at the battle for human dignity regarding civil rights and the giants that have gone down in history in that fight.

"The ugly there came to a head with Jimmie Lee Jackson. After he got out of the Korean War, he spent some time in Indiana before he went back home to where his mother and his grandfather were. He was killed being a part of a peaceful march in 1965, and his murder was the spark for the Selma-to- Montgomery march that Dr. King led. All of that started in Marion. My wife didn't leave there until she was a teenager, and although a child at the time, she remembers the march. She vividly recalls the night that Jimmie Lee Jackson was killed, and it was a pivotal moment in her childhood and in our history.

"With Jackson being in his early- to mid-twenties when he died, his only crime was that he wanted to exercise his right to vote after protecting our country. He died practicing his human dignity in the area of voting. Growing up, I was faced with the realism that such hateful places existed, especially in connection with my mother, my wife, my grandmother, and me. To me, as a child looking at it through their experiences down there, I understood that hate and racism were real. It is one thing to read about it; it is another to talk with those who lived through it. Once I became an adult, I would find myself in that environment where I was able to pick it up for myself. Even when nothing was said or done to me directly, it was the spirit of it I felt. I was aware of not only what I saw in the physical environment but what I internalized—the impressions of hostility and bitterness from Caucasian people there. I would mesh that with what my mother had told me from her childhood.

"I also couldn't get out of my mind the pictures of Bloody Sunday and what happened to our people there—people like Jimmie Lee. I saw a blaring contradiction. If you have such a heart for protecting education, that aspect of human dignity that brings forth potential, then where was that heart when it came to the lynching and the murdering? What about the hostility toward their destiny and their future, even beyond education, such as at the ballot box?

"So that's why I call it a paradox or a contradiction

because depending on how you're looking at it, you see undeniable beauty on one side because education is a work of art. Then to see the castration of that potential by actions that negate that education is horrible. All because they wouldn't let that same potential exercise its human right to vote or to shape the future with knowledge. It's interesting. I don't believe I would have come to that place or synergy had it not been for this book and preparing to be interviewed. I know now I needed this as an educator because these are my roots, and this is what I became as a result of them.

"For so long as a kid, I would go back almost every summer to spend time with my grandmother when she wasn't coming up here to Indiana. When I became older, moving into my teens, I didn't want to go back. Even though I still have family there, I just didn't believe it was worth the discomfort of having to be there. It's been twenty-something years since I went, and I spoke one weekend there, and I have not had a desire to return. I admit it was because I could not get over that unsettling and disheartening feeling, the sickness in my stomach even just driving down Highway 5 from Birmingham after getting off Highway 65, just coming into Marion. I could just imagine my people walking through the oppression, disenfranchisement, and the marginalization that was forced on them. For those people who refused or resisted—and there are a lot of them who did—they stayed, and they fought.

"Yes, things have changed, but in my mind, I'm still stuck in the past. I still remember things like my mother and grandmother warning me when I went down there. 'Oscar, baby, don't look those white people in the eyes. If they ask you something, be polite,' they would say. Into my teens, when I visited there, one of my uncles or my aunts made sure they were always with me. I resented being told as a kid that you have to show this respect to protect your life. I know my mother and grandmother were only trying to preserve something in me the world was going to need one day.

"I guess now, I needed to get this closure, and I needed to extract from the bitter, the sweet, such as the things that God has blessed me to do in education with so many young people. I must give some credit to the foundation of my roots and to the beautiful part of Marion with its historical passion for educating African Americans. I have been told repeatedly by relatives, 'It's different now; it's different.' I'm going to have to test it. I'm going to have to go back at some point. There is progress to meet, like my wife's nephew, who is a pastor there but was also one of the former sheriffs of Perry County. For him to have been elected, that really told me things. At least the voting components are no longer where most African Americans are denied their ability (and even killed over it). That he could ascend to a position like that and those that made it on the town council and so forth shows me that obviously, there is progress, and I applaud Marion for that.

"History is history, and to know that they've passed through and that's no longer commonplace there gives me comfort. When you look at the entire landscape of the history of those experiences that our ancestors there went through, you see that is a part of us. It's the part that explains what I am doing in education, now in my forty-seventh year of bringing forth the incredible academic potential in young people—of every race. It explains what Mathew has been doing all his life and how he developed the potential in so many people, including his daughters, and what they pass on as inspiration to others.

"When reminded, 'Oscar, we need to go back down there together and just take a tour, to walk around and just see our roots,' I remember thinking to myself about why I haven't I gone back over the years. I was too busy pursuing a difference in education in Indiana to have to go put up with the drama, the foolishness that racist spirit down there held.... I just decided that I did not want to put myself or my family in that position anymore. I asked myself if it was possible that the driving force in me, the hunger that makes me unable to stand not seeing any young person achieve, the fire that makes me especially reach for those who have been written off by society…could that have something to do with the beautiful part of Marion, Alabama, and its historical commitment to the education of African American kids?"

PART II
GROWING UP
GADSDEN

NAME CALLING & B-BALLING

In looking at Marion's emphasis on education, even during such racially charged times as after the Civil War, it's incredible how hard we had to fight for equal access to it in my hometown of Gadsden, Alabama. The city has a distinction of being the location of one of the largest demonstrations ever held—North or South—in the civil rights movement. I find many threads from my growing up there, including my family life, woven to form the picture of my adult life—from my puberty years with all the defiance, the risks, and the traumas I experienced and from the people of the town, as far back as the Native Americans who were removed from it so we could all live there. They all formed the pieces, particularly in my school years, of the future me.

The layout of Gadsden's residential community was unique, making the white and black lines between the residents there an odd mix. For example, there was the house my parents built on a small plot of land facing a field with a fence of trees shielding the white neighborhood on the other side. There was not one designated side of town for each race. The street where black people lived might just end where white households would begin. Several blocks down, another black neighborhood would begin. The only obvious "black people don't go there" line seemed to start once you hit a certain part of Rainbow Drive, which runs through the middle of the city. I never drove over that bridge or into Rainbow City to see how that side of town lived until 2017.

For the community where I grew up, this made boundary lines where you went to school confusing in the days before we integrated them. Only after returning in 2017 did all the pieces come together for me in Gadsden. In a trip there, I sought the recollections of relatives. Because of his remarkable journey and how he and his family made verifiable changes to the town, I called on my first cousin Robert Avery. His childhood participation in the civil rights movement is the stuff of legends. It led to a lengthy recognition by former President Barack Obama at the Forty-Third Annual Legislative Conference in 2013.

I sought his memories as well as my sister Chiquita's, both current residents of Gadsden, to help weave this section together. Here, the first piece begins not with my family but with school, where I learned how to see the racial lines for myself and learned how and when to step over them. I find it fitting, now that I am a college professor, to trace my academic life through my education during the country's most racist climate. As a student, I became a tool of defiance when it came to getting a fair shot at learning.

The 1954 ruling that struck down segregation in public schools as unconstitutional took place just two years after I was born with *Brown v. Board of Education of Topeka*. By the time I was heading into middle school in Gadsden, Alabama, the effort to carry it out was still blocked throughout the South. Schools in Alabama suffered from that racially segregated environment.

Like in Marion, using Oscar's analogy, we often see the tale of two cities, with progress and racism both running neck and neck. Like much of the South, Alabama continued to contradict itself by pushing to fix underfunding problems and salaries for teachers, yet they kept passing segregationist laws and simultaneously enabling the racists behind them. The 1955 Pupil Placement, and other laws passed in 1956, allowed school boards the power to resist desegregation. For example, they could shut down (or move so far away that the integrators would give up) any school getting those efforts. Then, the ruling that most affected where I ended up going to school was the Freedom of Choice Law. It was to allow parents the power to decide where we would attend. The freedom was a matter of where they would have you, and the choice part meant: *You can try and go over there if you want to and face God-knows-what when you get there.* They knew full well the often-disastrous reception we would receive at heavily segregated schools.

With separate education for white and blacks, it's no wonder any number of private schools popped up that could further draw the lines. How my parents afforded private Catholic school for me is a wonder by itself. St. Martin de Porres, where I went, was only grades one to eight. This meant my parents (mainly my mother) were forced to decide where I went next in the middle of rampant desegregation.

Even though George Wallace, as acting governor, offered us so-called Freedom of Choice, it was no choice at all for some of us. It didn't happen that the ruling passed one day and then all little black kids got to go to school wherever they chose the next. It was a sluggish movement in places with complicated and forced decisions based on things like available transportation and quality of education once you got there. Alabama schools did not begin true integration efforts until 1963—almost a full decade after the rulings and with daily resistance for every year in between throughout the South. It took people like attorney Fred Gray and a lot of beaten-in heads behind those civil rights cases to drive the decision home there.

It took another two years and at least one bloody summer in 1963 to see any genuine change in the structure of desegregation. We had more than a few foes to that freedom besides Governor Wallace. In '63, most memorably for me, Colonel Albert J. Lingo and his infamous state troopers rode in to town. He was the muscle behind Wallace's campaign pledge: "Segregation now! Segregation tomorrow! Segregation forever!"

My parents knew the deal, and my mother was one of

the many who decided they didn't like that and weren't planning on taking it sitting down. To show how popular Wallace and his racist ideas were—as a reflection of the era—by 1968, he became a well-supported third-party candidate in the presidential campaign representing the American Independent Party. He gained a position on ballots in all fifty states, which was more than any other third-party candidate in history. With a total of 9.9 million popular votes, we can use that number as just a fraction of the resistance we black kids who needed a good education faced.

The Freedom of Choice setup made it much easier for my parents to decide where I would go. Based on the simple fact that I lived in East Gadsden, when it came to schools, my choices were few. What made sense was that I would go to Litchfield Junior High. My mother (I don't remember my dad ever having or putting in much say about my school decisions), along with a few other parents, decided to change things. They got an idea that I would join a handful of other students and integrate Litchfield. At age thirteen, I can't say I had any power to resist. Neither did I have a clue as to what I would face as one of a half-dozen black kids in such a large, all-white school.

Mama started preparing me that summer. As a proud woman, she didn't want me to go and look any different regarding dress. My parents worked very hard with Green Stamps and shopping at Sears and Roebuck to buy some nice clothes for me that year. Any hesitation I felt about going to Litchfield was met with, "You will be going to school there. Period." My mother wasn't the type of woman who would allow her kids to play into a decision at that age. It was her way and no other way. She got that from her mother, and with that same fire, she was determined to see the integration of that all-white school, mainly because it made the most sense—Wallace and his 9.9 million racists be damned.

The first day of school was frightening for me. Picture six of us black kids integrating Litchfield's tally of over six hundred white kids. That first day of just walking in the hallways was scary because I had never been in an environment that large. St. Martin de Porres held one hundred students at most, and I stayed in the same class all day long. At Litchfield, for the first time, I changed classes. I never even knew what the homeroom concept was until then. Not only was I among the first to break a color barrier, but I was also breaking in aspects of myself for the first time too. It was hell —that feeling of anxiety I had the day before school started over the anticipation of what to expect.

That first day began with us greeted by angry white parents outside and angry white students inside. My nightmare commenced in Mr. Jones's eighth grade English class. I remember standing up to read the paragraph and making a mistake and all the students in the class laughing me into humiliation. In the beginning, there were many moments like these—and not just for me but for the other five black classmates as well. Keep in mind also, the white kids there had no doubt already been taking classes together for two years before I got there, and they had already experienced the culture of Litchfield. I can't speak for the other five black kids integrating with me because I don't know exactly where they went their first two years of junior high, and don't know if they had similar experiences or not. I just know mine was intimidating.

Is bullying any different in school when it has racial undertones? I think it affects you the same no matter who is doing it for whatever reason. When you *know* they are doing it because of your color and are encouraged by parents and some teachers in it, how can it not cut deeper into you as a kid? You can get better clothes, clean up pimples, or even change your weight to outgrow the insults. Perhaps even change your skin color if you bleach it enough, but your authentic race won't change. *You* won't change, and perhaps neither will they. If generational lessons in hate are at the root of their bullying, you can expect to dig in for the long haul. As in my case, you might eventually develop skin thick enough to withstand a trooper's electric cattle prod.

I was tall, dark, and skinny, but there was this one goofy kid who was a lot taller and paler. In fact, he was the tallest kid at the school and the resident class clown. Have you ever seen the TV show *Everybody Hates Chris*? Well, that would be me at Litchfield. I was the same kind of nerdy kid getting harassed left and right at school. The hallways were where I had the most negative experiences with this one kid. Laughing and knocking the books out of my hand, he, and the others like him, would get around me. That was for warmups. Getting shoved, tripped, stuff thrown at you, whether spitballs, sharpened pencils, or insults with the N-word spat out like bubblegum at your feet—all of that was common for integrating children. It was no different for me. Because she feared the way I might otherwise be treated, my mother took a job in Litchfield's school cafeteria. She was "gonna keep an eye on me." Because she had fought to get me in there, she took the only job she could get to be close and make sure I was okay there. My mother was always involved with the school; I don't know if my dad ever came to any of my three schools because he was always working. I do know he would listen to the basketball games, and when I played in high school, he would record them, but he never attended a game at all.

The distance from Litchfield to my house was about a ten- to fifteen- minute drive, but it was a very long one-hour walk, especially alone with that kind of treatment following you around. It got downright scary when one of the kids bullying you bragged that his folks were in the Klan and they had told him to give us black kids hell. It became smarter to travel in numbers.

There was a somewhat affluent black neighborhood not far from the school where two of the kids lived. One of them, L. C., had a dad who was the basketball coach at the all-black school there, Carver High. L. C. played on the basketball team at our school, and I would go to his house after classes. From there, my parents would come and pick me up, or I would walk home. The other integrating student was a young lady, Barbara Carstarphen, who lived the next block over from L. C. It also made it safer for her to walk home. Later, we all began attending Gadsden High together. There, we maneuvered around much of the same harassment we had at Litchfield.

L. C. was the one who first suggested basketball to me at Litchfield. I was not good at it at all, but because I was tall, the coach also approached me about trying out. Yes, it's a stereotype, but the assumption was if you're tall and you're black, you've got to be able to play ball. I couldn't. I was the kid who was the last to be picked on the playground with even the black kids playing basketball—that's how bad I started out.

I ended up being the last kid to make the list for the team. The coach told me the reason he let me on at all was that when he told me to change a specific technique, I did it immediately, and he recognized the potential in that. He said he saw some opportunity and that I could get better. In the end, that is how I made the team—because I was tall and black with potential.

I got much better and eventually became the star in high school. One thing I realized as I started to improve was I was treated significantly better by the white kids. Where before I was ignored completely, somebody might say "Hello" or even "Hi, Mathew" after that.

There were white students who crossed the line in getting to know me at that point, especially some of the girls, but that is a later chapter. There was still plenty of hostility as far up as the teachers. I don't even know if they have shop in schools today, but back then, shop taught you how to craft things. It was a class favored mostly by the poor kids in my school, who were probably not thinking of seeking higher education and wanted a local trade. Both the teacher of the shop class and many of the students were ones coming from the rural areas with backgrounds in deep southern prejudice.

In shop class, I experienced a teacher who treated me terribly by talking to the other students as if I weren't in the room, not even looking at me or touching me if he had to hand me something. If I got to see his eyes at all, they showed me how he felt about my being one of those "firsts" at Litchfield. If one of those farm boys had taken a two-by-four to my head, even then, I don't know that this teacher would have looked my way.

Mr. Jones was just the opposite. As my English teacher, he was a kind man. Here is another time when the lines between these contrasting examples of humanity thin out and show both the ugly and the beauty side by side. My English teacher was a man who saw his students as human beings and nothing else, versus the shop teacher, who was no less white but couldn't muster up enough compassion to even look me in my eyes, and I was a student—a child!

Here is how such hateful racism can plant seeds of trauma: I don't even remember the evil shop teacher's name, yet I do Mr. Jones and only one or two other teachers who were kind—all others have been blotted out. I don't even pull a visual of any of the other classes in my head. Looking through my old photos, such as me playing basketball during those years, it brought back a flood of memories, but only a few educators stand out. From primary school at St. Martin de Porres to college, this look at how one teacher's mistreatment stood out had me reflect on whether my quality of education was ever affected by this subtle racism.

Over my academic timeline, I could identify how the teachers and the choice of schools planted specific impressions. St. Martin de Porres was a private Catholic elementary school where the priest and all the Dominican nuns (who were quite abusive) were white. I was an altar boy in the church adjacent to the small school as well. I didn't imagine then that there were any black Dominican nuns there. There was still a degree of discrimination in that the majority of those students were Catholics, and by far, they got treated differently from those few of us who were not.

It should be noted that the quality and treatment from teachers is the first human contact outside of family a child gets. If they are cruel or racist or strict for no other reason than pushing a student to excel, then they plant seeds of trauma. Because life's fabric has in it patches of positive, like Mr. Jones among others, I progressed with excellent grades through school on into advanced degrees later in life. I can say that many did hand me racism with my ABCs, but they didn't manage to cripple my capacity to learn.

By the time I went to high school, thanks to Freedom of Choice, we had three to choose from around us. There were Emma Sampson and Gadsden High, which had majority all-white students, and then Carver, the all-black high school (where my cousin Robert Avery and his brothers attended). Emma Sampson was a lot further than the others. It was definitely because of my mother's involvement in the desegregation movement that I was going to be placed somewhere as an example, but I would also go where it was convenient since we lived so far.

My mother was certain that I was not going to Carver High School at that time. I agreed with that because I was comfortable by then with those white kids at Litchfield, and I was finally even getting a certain amount of respect. Because I was treated better, I found a slow acceleration from junior high up to my tenth-grade year on the basketball team as well. Once I got some position there, with my mother nearby watching my back, I got comfortable in that majority all-white atmosphere of learning. It was going to be hard to walk back through a community that had started calling me "Oreo."

About that time, an interesting event was happening in Gadsden, and I'm certain it probably happened throughout the South. The board of education would go into the black schools (in our instance it was Carver High), get three of their best teachers, and send them over to Gadsden High. Then they sent three of their worst white teachers over to Carver. So oddly enough, my very first black teacher was at Gadsden High.

I remember her like yesterday. She was young and had no order in her class. We did what we wanted to, but unlike her, the other black teachers, like my English teacher in her late twenties to early thirties, were very strict and took no nonsense in their rooms. My history teacher was also strict. She pushed us hard because she wanted us to excel. I was good at math, and the types of teachers I had made the difference because I made excellent grades in that subject. Yes, academically I was sailing and athletically I was too, but socially with my people, however, I was slowly sinking.

Every morning during my senior year of high school, we would recite the Pledge of Allegiance to the flag, and after that, they would call out the mail. It was a big deal if they said, "Mathew Knowles, we have mail in the office for you." That meant there was a college sending a letter, and that just made my major star power rise even more in school. I got a lot of attention, especially during my senior year and some during my junior year of high school. As I became a star player, life changed for me at Gadsden High while life became hell for me with my own people.

That's where the rip in the fabric began for me socially

—when I felt forced to stand on only one side of those lines. The problem was, no side seemed to want me. "Oreo" became a term for all black kids who went to a white school and mixed in their world. Students who didn't, and the folks who I knew in the community who just didn't like the idea of integration, called us that. Not everybody was down for stirring up trouble with white people to begin with because jobs and positions were on the line. But before long, I was wearing my school's orange and black jacket and colors, and by doing something so simple, I was alienating myself from my own racial peers.

Before I graduated, there was an event at Carver High that I attended and almost got my butt kicked. This kid wanted to fight just because I went to Gadsden High, and I just barely got away from a confrontation that day. Another time, I was going to a party and almost got jumped again. I was crazy enough to wear my jacket to the party and almost got beat up; it would have been ugly if I didn't run so fast. After that, I didn't go to any parties or events held by the black kids to avoid a fight. From a social standpoint for me, this treatment began a period of sadness because I couldn't go to any black social gathering, and I never got invited to any white ones. I absolutely wouldn't even think about dating a black girl from Carver and never did. The first thing that came to mind was that I would not have been stupid enough to do that based on what had happened. I just knew I would've gotten my butt kicked.

The South, and I know for sure my community, had a tremendous competition in sports. My cousin Robert's brothers —two of them— played for Carver High, which was one of the teams my high school competed against in basketball. In 2017, I asked Robert if he remembered that one night when all hell broke loose—the night we beat them in a game. "You mean the night y'all cheated," he joked.

I will let him give his childhood recollection of the era,

but his comment brought up more memories of what happened during the subsequent riot. That night of the game with Carver High, my Oreo status had me running right into one of my life's biggest ironies. As soon as the game ended and we players from Gadsden High were heading to our cars, the Carver students started a small riot. Black folks all around us were turning over several cars, and it was an angry, mob-like mess within an hour. It got so bad that the police and the state troopers came.

The irony is that the same troopers who beat my ass when I was protesting years before had to save it from my own people. Where we exited from the gym, we had to go out of the back door leading to the football field. That is where the state troopers all came in and stayed there with us until they got some order that night. I didn't quite understand why my people were including me in their rage just because I played for the white school. I knew then I had crossed over some invisible line, and that night, I would say I felt shoved over it by that irony. I got riskier and more daring while facing the line once I knew I had no other safe side to run behind anymore.

Those school years taught more than academics. I learned sometimes white kids were the enemy, sometimes they were just your schoolmates (or secret girlfriends if you could get away with it), and sometimes even the men who beat you were the shiny helmets that could come to save you. It was a twisted era.

My fellow student at Gadsden High, Barbara Carstarphen, was there as a witness to that era. She vividly recalls the impact we made there.

—Barbara Carstarphen-Bush
"I tell young people it wasn't just Rosa Parks but many others who were a part of that integration. My mother wanted

us to have the best. She was very forward thinking. We knew the schools we had never got the same supplies and materials as the all-white schools. We also wanted a gym and other amenities, but they didn't put the same money into ours. We loved our community's schools and teachers and felt nurtured by them. We understood it took a village to raise a child, but we also knew how they were limited.

"I had a civics class teacher who is the perfect example of the atmosphere at that time. She would purposely say 'Nigra' instead of Negro. I was in the eighth grade, but it was the first time I felt I should stand up for myself. There were only two of us black kids in the class. I raised my hand and explained it was very offensive, that pronunciation of Negro. She turned beet-red in the face, and for about a week she refrained. It didn't last long because by the end of that week, she was back to using it. They didn't want us there, and that was one way we knew it."

***

I am glad to have a witness like Barbara, not only to help recall those troubled moments but also the fun times we had in our childhood. Youth will persist, even in a tense and unwelcoming atmosphere. Eventually, it will push itself around any limitations to have as much fun as everybody else. Sports, entertainment, dating—whatever other kids were into, we as black kids sought it as well. In this, we forged our way into their yearbooks and history books in fair pursuit of our own adventures. I had been a soldier in a battle against discrimination before I was even in high school, so I managed to find my moments to enjoy my youth those last years as much as possible, like when a few of my friends and I got together and performed "Psychedelic Shack" by the Temptations for the school's talent show.

Those showcases were a big deal then, and everybody

wanted to go to one. We decided we were going to be the Temptations because we all liked their music and style. We had help from watching shows like *Soul Train*. In my house, we put aluminum foil on our TV antenna so we could get that station, and that helped me during my one big performance. Studying their act meant we had the image together, and I mean we had it down! We were confident that we were going to win, and we did, but we worked for it. We practiced and decided we were going to do this right, and so we rehearsed and rehearsed until we won. I learned that method back then and used that discipline in guiding acts in my later career. The music stayed and played subtle roles throughout my life.

Those good memories fill in the sore spots of those experiences I had during my away games when playing basketball at all-white schools. Those games were an exercise in overcoming fear—and yet still being good enough to win. They were going to harass us anyway, so the least we could do was beat the hell out of them. There were times that we would drive out immediately after a game. Being the only black people there, and it was only one or two, at most three of us that senior year, we had reasons to be nervous.

As the only black kids out there on a basketball court with nothing but one hundred percent amped-up white people in the crowd, we were getting called every name in the book. These were nasty insults, but being outnumbered, even if we were mad enough to show a reaction, there was nothing we could do, so we put our energy into beating their butts on the court. From the beginning of the game when we went out to warm up to the end when we were running into our dressing room and then onto the bus, we were operating in fear. And we were still expected to help our white teammates win the game. Can you imagine that?

One white man, our coach, was motivating us to win at all costs while almost one hundred more were hurling negativity as fast as we could move the ball. It did not get better in those small towns as far as racial hatred toward us players, even after seeing us black athletes repeatedly playing at those schools through the years. It was ingrained hate for them, and that meant it probably was too dangerous to hang around there after we were done.

Classmate Barbara Carstarphen also recalls those games and the hostile greetings we got when away from home:

—Barbara Carstarphen-Bush

"We thought it was important to support our team at those away games because you can only imagine what they had to endure. One of my friends had a car, and we'd go out to watch Mathew and the others as much as we could. They should have been scared to even win in places like Albertville, where our parents talked about black people lynched. Those areas were ones our folks were afraid for us to go to, so we didn't tell them where the game was so that they wouldn't worry. The black basketball players were called names and talked down to by the white people at the games, so we knew they needed all the support they could get. We thought they were the greatest. Three of the five stars on the team were black, and we had a lot of winning seasons. I remember one day, it was one girl's birthday, and Mathew told her he would get seventeen points because she was turning seventeen that day—and he did!

"However, the school spirit at pep rallies was hard because the school always played 'Way Down South in Dixie,' and students ran around waving Confederate flags. I felt there should only be the American flag there. Me and a core group of the four to five percent of blacks from that second year of integration got together, and I drafted a letter to the principal. It explained how we thought the song and the flags were offensive to us and that they should be discontinued. If they didn't, we would not participate in the pep rallies. He suggested they would play any song we wanted and said, 'You all can have "We Shall Overcome" or something that is important to you, but that song is important to us, and we want our song. If you walk out, you jeopardize scholarships or risk being kicked out.'

"We told Mathew and the other ballplayers we didn't expect them to take those risks, but the rest of us walked out and stood around the flag outside. They called our parents, and even the police came. The white students were in shock because I don't think they expected us to do anything or stand up for ourselves. They saw we were serious, and after that letter and us walking out, the school never played that song again.

"We were there growing up in a time when we were waking up in many ways during 1969 to 1970 when James Brown's 'Say It Loud—I'm Black and I'm Proud' revolutionized everything. The image of the beauty queen changed overnight to dark skin and afros. We became proud. That's how I remember Mathew as a tall, always well-dressed, proud, and intelligent young athlete. We were all there bringing in that revolution in our own ways during those years."

***

Barbara witnessed how rough it was to play ball as a teenager under those racist conditions. I had started to become more sensitive to racism even when it was subtle. It was hard to shake off the insults thrown while trying to maneuver that ball and then sit in class with them and still feel equal. They let us into their desks and schools—seldomly into their inner lives. My eyes and ears naturally sharpened because of those moments.

Just like Barbara, I had my own experience with how a

teacher pronounced Negro—but in their twang version that smacks of old-boy racism in the South. As seniors, we might have had maybe seven or eight black people, including two of my teammates and me in class where, oddly, the teacher was also our coach. Anytime he got to the word "Negro," he would say "Nigra" instead, in the way that was quite popular back then for white folks. I would talk about it with the other black players on the team, but we were too frightened of him to challenge him on why he would say it that way in class.

Years later, I uncovered something else this same coach did that if I had known might have changed my destiny. About fifteen years ago at Alabama A&M in Huntsville, I was there with a Destiny's Child concert when a much older man approached me and introduced himself. "I just wanted to say hello to you. I never did understand why you never got back to me. All those letters I sent to you on how I wanted you to play basketball here at Alabama A&M. I wondered why you never got back to me."

I was stunned because I remembered the excitement of mail call from the office at school, telling me schools eager for me were writing. I said I had no idea what he was talking about. "I never got one letter from you, ever." He insisted though. "Oh yeah, a lot of black schools were after you, Knowles. You don't know?" I couldn't believe it and told him so. "No, I never got any letters from black colleges. I only got them from white colleges." That's when I learned that same coach hid the fact those schools wanted to recruit me to play basketball. I would have at least visited because I was open. I never got the invites thanks to a man who couldn't even pronounce the race of the student he was holding back.

It added to the pressure of going into adulthood under the shadow of that kind of sneaky discrimination. The summer after high school, I wanted freedom from both my parents' house and the town. I was ready to drop street names like

Tuscaloosa Avenue from my memory because they troubled some part of me. They helped me remember pain and suffering, plus all the challenges I had moving through my childhood there. I just never wanted to go back. I had these negative feelings in my soul whenever I thought back to it. It is only apparent now with a retro look at how that racist climate shaped not just me but the parents who raised me.

MRS. KNOWLES

A man is not a complete picture without his bloodline. My teen rebellion led to the desertion of all things Gadsden once I left for college. That included my kinfolks for a while. I know that my parents were a major piece of my fabric. I can't leave my memories of Gadsden and its atmosphere in that era without a look at how they also maneuvered through it. Having faced even rougher times than I would, I couldn't then appreciate the strength I inherited from my parents, which helped me through that twisted era.

By now, I know those expressions of tough love, pride, and lessons of racial dignity were tools meant to be used in life. When I left Gadsden, I rarely spoke to my parents as a young adult. I missed years where their story was still being played out while my sister Chiquita was still there, growing up and getting her own version of life in the South as a Knowles.

It took a family investigation to help me realize why I needed to include the backdrop of my parents and grandparents in these pages. Whatever they experienced, we inadvertently inherited. Everything they absorbed on racism from how people could treat you to how to live with hatred, they passed on to us. They learned negative traits also, such as colorism from white slave masters, using it to separate us— like favoring lighter-skinned, silky-haired looks over others.

In examining who my mother was as far as personality, I can get why I ended up integrating an all-white middle school. Looking at my father, I see my entrepreneurial determination in vivid colors. By understanding the atmosphere in which they did all this, I can admire them that much more because it was a hardscrabble life sometimes. Although my mother worked as a colored maid for three dollars per day, it never took away her dignity as a black woman. Respect was something she demanded and received. I learned a lot from her early on, and a few incidents stand out on how she stood up to the racial climate with her back straight and little to no visible fear.

One example is when a white insurance salesman came to our home to collect the weekly premium. It was his first time there, and when he knocked on the door, he asked for "Helen." My mother promptly asked him to get back in his car and said, "When you can get out and ask for Mrs. Helen Knowles, I will speak with you. If not, please cancel my policy." He got back in his car, got out of it again, and came to the door with both an apology and a request to speak with "Mrs. Helen Knowles."

There was another time where she showed me her grit and strength. Since we lived in East Gadsden, the poor undeveloped area, my mother would occasionally catch the bus and take me with her. One time, the bus was full, so my mother and I stood in the front—or the "white section," as it was identified. Since there was an empty seat, and as a kid not understanding segregation, I just sat in it. That's what empty seats are for, aren't they?

The entire bus laughed at me, but my mother did not. She was busy glaring down the bus driver. "My son is not getting up!" she told him, and I think the tone of her voice and that icy glare convinced the driver not to combat her. I'm telling you Helen Knowles did not play, but she knew when to pick her fights and was incredibly brave through some of the scariest moments I can remember. One night is pivotal and stands out like it was yesterday.

For this, I'll have to take you back with me to my time at St. Martin de Porres Catholic school. Only it was to the church, where I was an altar boy, that we were headed on not just any night—it was Christmas Mass, which started at midnight. That mystical late hour in the ceremonial atmosphere of the Catholic church was a big deal for a kid, especially for the one who got to sing "O Holy Night," so you can imagine my surprise when I was selected for this honor. It's easy to forget, having spent so many years since then building up other singers (including daughters Solange and Beyoncé), that I ever did any singing myself. That night, I was the star attraction, so it was important I get there. After getting all ready, I was excited and well-dressed. Everybody was proud of me, and I was ready to go and do my best. It was only my mother driving just us two to Mass, and we set out late with this being midnight service. In her rearview mirror, she kept noticing the same truck following us as it tailed us some distance. This locale was back roads with no lights in mid-'50s rural Alabama. Do you get the picture?

I watched her do some strategic turns to see if the truck was indeed following us. It was. That's when that look, that grit I mentioned, hit her face. The quick-thinking Mrs. Helen Knowles didn't cower even then. Still, the incident showed my young eyes how fast fear and danger could rise up at any moment, and if it did, so must you. She decided to drive the car through several neighborhoods until we got to what was considered the projects, thick with black folks. She stopped at the only light there and got out screaming loud as hell. I saw the truck drive on by with three white men—disappointed, I'm sure—accelerating away in it.

Looking back, I see she was tough, but then she was born from a tougher era. I also see that I come from people more than complex than I ever realized as a child. Since a thorough portrait of a person is a more honest one, I asked my sister to also share her memory of growing up Gadsden and those years in the South with the infamous Mr. and Mrs. Knowles.

—Chiquita Knowles-Ash

"To me, my mother had a rough life. She grew up in the country on a farm. Since her daddy was a bootlegger and made that corn whiskey, they had to work the stills and do a lot in the fields. Since Mama didn't have a lot, she wanted the best for her children. I think that's why she gave my brother Mathew some of the principles he has. You know, 'Do the best; reach for the stars.' But her own life was never easy.

"Daddy was her second husband after her first husband left her and our older brother Jesse. I know for a fact that hurt her bad. Daddy had a big heart and was a hard worker, so maybe they saw they would do well together. They got married and even hand-built their own house by themselves after daddy bought some land. It had peach and apple trees on it, and Mama used them for canned fruit. She did a lot to keep her house together, but she wasn't as easygoing as Daddy. Some people used to say she was a hell-raiser, but she just wanted things right. She grew up working hard, so she got work cleaning houses for the white families. Some days, she would leave one job cleaning house, then go to another one and either clean it or tend other people's children. In her own time, she sewed and made beautiful quilts, and she loved to cook! She used to say, 'That's how you show love—through your food.'

"I remember waking up on Sunday morning to listen to a lot of gospel music or Mama in the kitchen cooking and singing old hymns like 'What a Friend We Have in Jesus' while she would fix the food. Daddy also loved to cook, and if Mama was out working late during the week, he would come home and do it. But Sunday was her day to fix us that big Sunday meal, and the best times were listening to music and her singing, plus smelling all that good food.

"As far as a couple, she would do her duties as a wife and a mother, and Daddy was the man of the house. But she didn't take mess from even him. Mama didn't care about his size; she wasn't scared of him. She would fuss whenever she felt like it, and she fussed a lot! Mama seemed like she stayed fussing at Daddy about something. That's how she went so hard after civil rights; when she wanted something, she fought for it. Going to the meetings and the marches was because she was ready for change and was mad about it. Mama would work all day, maybe for five dollars cleaning a house. That's rough. And then she would have no way to get to work. My daddy drove his job's produce truck, but they didn't have a car a lot of the time. Mama would have to either walk to work, or if they managed to get a car, it wouldn't last that long. She had to get to work, and that's the only thing she knew how to do was to clean houses and cook.

"On the side, she used to cook school lunches and cater for the people that she cleaned for. Like when they'd have a big party, she would prepare all the food. When neither one of them were at work on Sundays though, that was the best time in our house. Daddy would be in his room listening to his

blues or whatever old school music was for us back then—
that's what he liked. Mama was gospel. Mathew used to sing
too; he could sing—he really could. And he would dance. We
all did. It was a lot of fun during those times for everybody.
Mama would be in her little world cooking and seemed happy
then too. Education was very important to her and Dad too
because they didn't have that much, so we had all kinds of
books in the house too; she liked us to read and better
ourselves. Books and music, good food, and everybody
dancing or singing on Sunday is what I remember as the
happiest times."

***

Like Chiquita, I remembered the music well—how after
Sunday dinner my parents would go into the living room, you
know, where most families had that plastic on their sofas and
that area you couldn't go into as a child. We had to go around
it if there was a way or suffer for it until Sundays when we
would go in and dance. My role at ten years old was to have a
nickel, a dime, and a quarter to put on the top of the needle
because the vinyl would have scratches on it. And so, my job
was to make sure I had the right-sized stack of coins on that
needle plus DJ the records. I had a playlist in my head of all
the ones everybody wanted, from Fats Domino to Peaches and
Herb's "Close Your Eyes"—my parents loved that song. Now,
my dad was a huge man, tall and big, but he could dance—I
mean *dance*. That was always a highlight.

Yes, I remembered the music, the dancing, singing, and
of course the food, but I interrupt my sister here to speak
beyond those basic aspects of who our family was. I know that
our memories weren't always the same, but side by side, they
both can sketch the people we loved with deeper dimension. I
had my heroic versions of my mom, but she was still a
complex woman. Anybody who carried on every day through
segregation, two marriages, three children, and the limits of

her education would be. If she could chill out and sing on Sunday and fuss all day on Monday, she was still a significant piece of who shaped us. I wanted a view of my mother behind the music, so to speak.

—Chiquita

"I know Daddy loved her. He would do little things—bring her stuff to the house; he would buy her stuff to put a smile on her face…that kind of love. He tried. She was just… well, people didn't love the same way as we do now. Mama wasn't that kind of person, even with her kids. For me, I had to find love in myself. She showed it in her ways, but it wasn't just out there like we do it now. Maybe it wasn't love at first sight for her and Daddy, but they stayed together and worked hard for us.

"There is one thing that happened—it's kind of funny now—but it'll show how she stayed outspoken and tough, even when she got older. One day, she was out hanging clothes when she and this other lady got into an argument. The lady told Mama to 'kiss her ass.' Mama told her, 'Yeah, okay. I'll meet you around the corner.' Can you imagine two old women in a street fight—in their fifties in the street rolling? Mama got her good, but Daddy came home telling her, 'You don't need to be out there doing stuff like that!' But that's just how it was up on that hill; they kept up drama. But she and Daddy would do anything for anybody, and I guess you can say she loved hard, in her way, and fought even harder too.

"Even when she got older and sick, she was hard to control; she went wandering off, confused a lot. That's why I say my dad died from a broken heart because he couldn't take care of her anymore. Mama got to where she would not stay at the house. She would leave. She had some episodes where she forgot where she was, so she was put in the nursing home. One thing is that my mom would always call on Jesus a lot. That was her favorite thing to say. Sometimes the only words she would say were 'Jesus, Jesus, Jesus.' Toward the end, she didn't know nobody's name. Not even that one.

"Daddy died first after we had to move her out of the house—I think from a broken heart. Then we had to take her out of the nursing home later and put her in senior housing, where she had her own room and everything. I would go by there and check on her, and one day they called me and told me that she wanted to sit on the front porch. When I got there, she was sitting out there in the rocking chair. She wanted to see her grandbabies, so I went and got my children and brought them to her. She knew their names, and she wanted to talk to her sons. I don't think she talked to their children; I think she just spoke to Mathew and Jesse on the phone.

"To me, that was like a miracle because this lady had no clue who anybody was for years. Then one day, she suddenly knows everybody's name! She had one clear day, and two weeks later, she passed. It could be hard growing up under her in that house; I can't lie. She was sometimes beyond hard on all of us. There was a lot to love about Mama; you just have to stop and think about it. I would have to say, I learned no matter what that family is important in the end. Because that's real love."

***

After getting my sister's point of view on my mother, it was time to look at my dad too. Seldom do children look for humanizing details in their parents, but adults sure do. My father offered yet another picture when it came to race relations growing up. One of his favorite jokes was: "The first day I went to school, they had no books. The second day, the teacher didn't show up. And the third day, the school burned down." That summed up his education, or lack of one, in one joke. Because he worked so much, I, unfortunately, didn't have the opportunity to spend as much time with him as my mother.

Both were some of my first mentors just because of the impressions they made.

His entrepreneurial legacy passed on to me and into my children, I am sure, just by his brilliant determination and creativity. An example is how he convinced his employer to let him keep the truck he drove delivering the local produce full time. Now he had ample access to a truck to use for his own affairs. He would go and tear down old houses and sell the lumber, and he would also collect metal—aluminum, copper, etc.—that he would sell. By taking the old cars from people's yards, he would then sell the old car parts— all for additional income. He stacked those broken-down buses and work sheds on the back of the property we owned with stuff that might be worth a fortune today as antiques.

Dad built not one but two houses there with his own hands from bricks and wood, renting out one next door and living in the other on the land until his last day. He was so big that he left an impression on everybody he met. Since he was such a giving person who believed in helping everyone regardless of color, it was something he always tried to instill in us too. After working two to three jobs per day, he still found the time to be a volunteer fireman. On those days, he would sit and listen to a CB radio to see if there was a fire in progress so he could go and help. I saw, through him, that despite the ones who wanted to keep you down, we all had to live alongside each other anyway. One man's fire was as good as another's if it burned your own house down.

Whether we had to put out one another's fires or eat each other's vegetables, it was one community tying us together once you got beyond the nameless borders. My dad knew fire lines didn't stop like we did—at the end of a block where a Confederate flag might wave from somebody's porch. Watching him work so hard yet so smartly, I came up knowing you didn't have just to sit and struggle. Because he worked so much and because I don't remember him participating in my school days or even the protests that Mom did, this left me with only those single frames of reference when I describe him: 'hard worker and good man.' Here was a man who lived through that racially charged time in Alabama. He had to have faced some trauma and felt something about it all too. He's gone now, and I can't ask him, but I can gather clues after the fact on him just like all the rest. That clue is like a puzzle piece fished from under an old sofa cushion, and I needed them all to complete the picture of not just him but the entire era.

I never needed to ask deeper questions about him because he seemed straightforward as a father figure and, as my sister called him, "a family man." I had traced a lot of my mother's temperament and hard work ethic to her mother and identified the Hogues as well as I could. However, the Knowles side, and how they handled those troubled times, would be another mystery, starting with my dad.

Prophet Isaiah Knowles and wife
Jane Hall Knowles
Far Right: Jane Hall Knowles
circa early 1900's

BIG MAC'S REVENGE

According to my cousin Robert Avery, the Knowles family name originated from the Bahamas, where you'll find the name extremely common. My father's grandparents, Prophet Isaiah and Jane Hall Knowles, strike a bold pose in family pictures. Living through the turn of the century, what might they have experienced during those times as a black couple in rural Alabama? And how curious to find possible Bahamian roots, and I wonder what sort of story waits behind such a discovery. Whoever the first Knowles ancestors in America were, they landed and began our family in Cherokee County. Digging into that part of my DNA is a current project of mine. The scant information I've gathered to date shows yet another proud bloodline of hardworking men and women whose true histories have been reduced to census footnotes and old photos. There are also our memories left, and I set about gathering those of my father's family also.

Dad's own mother, Girlie Mae Knowles, and my paternal family were renowned for cookouts held right in the backyard under two pecan trees. They were trees that my grandparents planted, and they now tower above the house with stories to tell. Across the street was a nightclub, the Royal Palm, which was a popular stop on the old "Chitlin' Circuit," as it was then called for black performers. Bobby Blue Bland, B. B. King, and others played there to a packed house, and when it was over, my grandmother offered after- hours liquor as well as home-cooked southern food that was legendary for miles.

The entertainers would hang around after and before shows, mixing with everyone just like family and exposing us kids to lasting memories. As Robert said, "We held more cookouts and did more fish frying under those trees than the law should allow." No wonder my father loved to dance to good music and was such a sociable man. Who was this gentle giant? Getting my sister's point of view helped me flesh out a portrait nearly as big as the man himself.

FROM THE EYES OF
CHIQUITA KNOWLES-ASH

"Daddy used to deliver the produce to people's houses. Any food they didn't sell or was going to go bad he would bring home or give away to all these different people in the neighborhood. That's why everybody trusted and loved him. One time, he went to this lady's door, and this man had been beating on her. Daddy went and found that man and pushed him down a couple of times. That's why I think they liked him helping put out all those fires—because he was big and because he had a big heart. Daddy was only a volunteer fireman, not one they had signed on the job and was paid like the other men. It was just something he wanted to do, but because of his race and because of his level of high school (I don't think he ever did graduate from elementary), he couldn't get the actual job title.

"He was a great firefighter, and he opened the doors because at that time we didn't have black firemen at all. But here was one who would just show up, and so they would give him the hose and stand back and let him help put the fire out. Because he was almost four hundred pounds and so tall, he could hold that hose down by himself. Imagine all those other firemen standing and watching this black man, who just showed up one day to help, holding down a water hose alone. It would take way more than one of them to do it, so think about that.

"Because he had a big heart, one time he went inside and saved a white man from a house that was burning down. At first, they couldn't get the man out of the house. Then, the other firemen just said, 'Forget it; don't go in there. .He's just a drunk.' My dad went in anyway and picked him up, threw him over his shoulder, and took him out of the house. It didn't matter if he was a white or black man. Daddy wouldn't have cared. He went to every fire there was, and the only thing they used to do for him was at Christmastime, they would pass the hat around, give him a little Christmas gift or something. Here he could hold that hose down himself, but they couldn't just go on and make him a real fireman. They knew he had that much strength in him, but they could only pass a hat.

"It didn't matter. That's something he did enjoy doing because he loved to help people. If you were walking down the street, he would give you a lift to where you had to go. A person like that has to be useful, and it's their nature. So the hat collection didn't matter. He would just be at the next fire, then the next one—working hard, carrying people out and stuff. That was how he was. If he knew about a family that needed food, he would drop it off at their house; he wouldn't even knock. There was this lady that said she was getting ready to go somewhere, and there was a box of food at her front door, and she just knew Daddy had brought it to her.

"That's why they did that article in the *Gadsden Times*. It said it right there in the headlines, 'Big Boy's Always There.' His name was Big Mac—that's what people called him, and yet they called him 'boy' in the paper—now that was racist. He was a grown man, and they would still call him 'Big Boy.' That's just disrespectful. Still, he always said, 'It's a person's heart that matters, not the color of their skin.' That's the way he raised us. He had a good heart, and it showed by the fact he always had a smile on his face. Yeah, Mama did give him hell, but he always looked happy.

"You can tell how he was because of how good he was with kids. He loved children, and every baby he saw, he would bounce them and sing to them. He used to call Beyoncé 'Bey' because he couldn't say Beyoncé well, so he just called her that. He also used to sing to her all the time, like all of his grandkids. I have a daughter about the same age as Beyoncé, and he would take both of them sometimes, one of them in each arm and just sing '…Daddy gonna buy you a mockingbird…,' and he would rock and sing them to sleep.

"He was funny too, like with some of the things he did and things that kept Mama fussing after him so much. Daddy was an original junkman. You know Sanford and Son? He was Fred Sanford on that fruit truck picking up things here and there while on the road. Either he would make something out of it, or he could sell it for junk. He loved to barbeque, and I remember that he had picked up a clothes dryer and turned it into a barbecue smoker. This was a long time ago before all these fancy grills they have now, but he turned this dryer into a smoker, and that's how he used to cook his meat. He found some use for everything he picked up. Mama couldn't take it sometimes though.

"I don't think it's that Daddy didn't get involved in all the marches and things Mama did—it's that he made his own changes and did what he wanted, which was just go help people anyway. He knew it was racism out there, but it never stopped him. I learned a lot from him about being positive and loving people regardless of their color. That's what he told me when I saw some racism at my school. He was trying to teach us to deal with it all. One particular time, I remember Daddy encouraging me after I experienced racism. Because my mama felt like we were supposed to make good grades in school, she wanted us to go to the best ones. Then they started desegregating them, so I had to go to an all-white school. It was like the teachers felt you couldn't be making good grades, like you were supposed to be dumb or something.

"I remember in the fourth grade this girl calling somebody the 'N' word, and the teacher corrected her by having her look it up to see what one was. In the dictionary, it said it was a low-class person. The teacher pointed out that that could be her or it could be anybody. It wasn't the color of the skin that made the person low class; it was things that person did that made them that way. This was a white teacher that pointed it out to the whole class. I thought that was a big thing. The girl had to stay after PE and write on the blackboard what it meant. What Daddy taught me helped me appreciate that lesson even more, but I could still see the differences, and as I got older, I felt it more.

"Once Mathew moved to Houston and I was a teenager, I was tired of all that. I wanted to be with my brother, I wanted to change my life, and I felt I couldn't get that opportunity or change in Gadsden. My mom, she was the sweetest person she could be at times, but remember she was a hell-raiser. She loved you with tough love, like 'knock you upside the head because I love you; you don't need to do that anymore' love. That's the way she raised us. She was tough on Mathew too, but he was gone, so I ran away. I had to come back home at some point, but after I graduated from high school, I left to go to Houston with Mathew. I stayed away a year. It was '79 and '80, and it was wild there during that time in that city. I mean, I was a country girl, so from country girl to Houston? It was something else. I came by Greyhound that first time. I flew back a couple of times, but I arrived by bus because I just wanted to get away from Gadsden.

"It was a learning experience leaving the South. Mathew helped me get a good job, and I was making pretty good money. Plus, I realized something I had learned from my mom —how to make some money by cooking. I would sell plates to a lot of Mathew's friends. I made good money on the side doing that. I enjoyed cooking, and since that was how Mama would say she was showing love, I did it too. But the city was too much and too fast for me, and I left to go back home after a while. I stayed in Gadsden this time and started a family. I got to be with my mom and dad to the end.

"Daddy was there for my kids from the start, and we used to talk every day. He would be there protecting me against all the bad things in life and helping me with the kids when I needed. I would come home, and Daddy would just be sitting on the porch waiting for me. I was his lil' girl, and he would be looking out for me. I could always count on him. Because he kept his pantry stocked like a grocery store, I would go over there and raid it. It felt good to know he was always there when I needed him. That's why it hurts me so bad to this day I wasn't there for him when he died.

"It was the first of the year with after-Christmas sales going on, so I was out shopping and didn't call Daddy that day. When I got home, the phone was ringing. I answered, and they told me my daddy had died. I remembered then that I didn't call him that morning. I did everything that day but call my dad, and it hurt me more to realize he had experienced a heart attack by himself. The ambulance got there, and they took him to the hospital alone. They had tried and tried to call me—this was before they had cell phones. They sent another crew to come and get me later. It just bothered me that Daddy died by himself. I wasn't there, and I didn't get to see him. I didn't get to hold his hand, none of that. He'd always been there for us, but when he had passed, I wasn't there for him. It still bothers me, but I know he loves me, and he knows I love him."

***

After hearing my sister's version, and in retrospect, I believe Mathew Knowles—Big Mac—got the last word. I call it Big Mac's revenge. I imagine great envy from some of those men watching him handle a hose as if he owned it. I know they wondered why somebody would give his all like that in their spare time. They knew he was special, and the article in the *Gadsden Times* was an attempt to express that. But those lines are there again, slicing between the ugly and the good intent. It's beautiful in that they thought enough to honor him in print in the first place after all those years, but the ugly is that "BOY." Is it too late to get a posthumous error reprint?

The laws and rules of his times said no black firemen existed. Apparently, to Big Mac that didn't matter, and he didn't bother to march for it or protest the case outside of a burning building. He just showed up, grabbed a hose, and called himself a fireman. And they let him year after year. He listened to that CB to find out where else he could be productive in the community. He went and put his whole back into it and didn't wait for them to permit him. He didn't care about their Christmas hat—he made his own money and still went and volunteered his free time.

This gentle giant had so many people loving him, and he is remembered as far as Birmingham just from those he serviced on his route, ones who appreciated his good nature. He is loved by the babies he rocked and tucked away with songs they still hum without them even remembering where the songs originated. We wake up the memory of Big Mac so all of his offspring and theirs can know him more. In memory, that gentle giant who didn't wait for what he wanted to be happy or free, will never be alone.

SUMMER 1963

Going back in time to 1963, while I spun in a daze with school, the civil rights movement was spinning around all of us. In my house, it started with my mother making moves like sending me to integrate a school. Education was important to her idea of getting far away from Marion and away from the struggles of living poor under some racist's thumb. Helen Knowles only got as far as the eleventh grade, which was good for those times, especially coming from a farm. She attended the same school as Coretta Scott King in Marion and later played her active role in desegregation in Gadsden by attending marches, sit-ins, and protesting injustice. By the time I came of age, I was with her doing the same.

Although designed for controlling cattle, the cattle prod I mentioned was used by the police in Alabama on demonstrators. I experienced it before I was old enough to shave. When the Birmingham church bombings happened, those of us in school that September 1963 were shook up emotionally as well. I was only eleven years old, but when the news of protests stirring reached us, we couldn't sit still. Knowing your mama, the church people, your older cousins, and your neighbors all were taking their upset to the streets, nobody wanted to sit with a pencil in their hand. Just knowing a city or two over some little girls my age had been killed by racist men while in church—it all came to a head in my mind too. I had already been rattled by personal events in my life the year before, and when I looked back, I realized that psychologically it made sense that I wanted to scream—and loudly too. Many other young people twenty-one and under must have needed to rebel yell that summer because, at its core, it was a youth movement. It was the Little Rock Nine kids, the Birmingham church bombing girls, and the college students taking direct hits, and we were spitting mad by 1963 in Gadsden.

My cousin Robert was arrested three times in one day as he'll explain in his own words. I remember running and reaching the railroad tracks behind the store where my father drove the produce truck. To the left and the right, troopers were coming with shiny helmets flashing in the sun. I could imagine what a deer feels like stuck in a headlight for a minute —that's how I saw them coming at us. One day, when I was running away from them and we got to the railroad tracks, we were stuck. We had nothing but woods to our backs, but on the other side waiting for us was Mt. Pilgrim, the church that hosted our marches for the movement there. You could go to the church to get your assignments on sit-ins, protests, and such. If you got bloodied up, that is where they patched you up and put you right back on the protest lines if you were willing. I often was willing that summer.

The day that the troopers caught me is when I met the brute force of racism, physically. A skinny eleven year old is nothing compared to a large bull, so a cattle prod should've hardly seemed necessary to stop me. When it hit me, I broke and cut through those woods, hurting like hell but running as fast as any deer, heading for the sanctuary of the church. You had the protection of church and home and school as a kid. If any of those were troubled, you could bet some part of you would also be. Piecing together our childhood, I would later have the tools to free the parts of me the court rulings never got to—ones that foreshadowed that ugly summer.

Remember: what children see helps shape their understanding of the world, themselves, and later their families. That is why studying the entire inner lining that makes up your childhood and the roles others played on your psyche can tell a lot about your adulthood later. As a native of Gadsden, I was born in time to see it still holding on to segregation with some tight hands. Once sit-ins at whites-only establishments started trying to loosen them, the arrests, hosings, beatings, and what looked like civil war to a young black man started. As a kid, I didn't know all the details of what led up to the movement; yet I knew enough from what I could see to participate. Only as an adult could I research and come across the many other back stories and threads that came together to start that volatile summer.

One I know now is that after a union steelworker, Joseph Faulkner, along with two others were arrested for a bus sit-in, they started the East Gadsden Brotherhood. This event stirred up movement among local students, church leaders, and community members. With marches and protests, including a major boycott of white merchants, our town picked up on what was happening in nearby Birmingham. In no time, high-profile supporters such as the Student Nonviolent Coordinating Committee (SNCC) along with the Congress of Racial Equality (CORE), and the SCLC came in with field secretaries.

Not to be stopped in their hate, Alabama state troopers began using a tool that I became painfully familiar with—the electric cattle prod. Even during our prayer vigils and among the most peaceful of protests, we were often surrounded and pounded by hundreds of armed officers. It didn't matter if your head was down praying and a baby slept in your arms or if you were carrying a baby in your belly with a picket sign in hand —into the dirt you went if Lingo and his boys had anything to say about it. We saw young people in Birmingham on the news chased and hosed down—and we're not talking sprinklings like on a wet lawn. These were full-pressure fire hoses like a bomb blast against your back. There's no standing on your feet when that stream hits you. Standing on our feet in life is why we, young and old, were out there despite snarling dogs and all.

The more the brutality took place, the more America began to wake up as more demonstrations started up in cities across the country—with both white and black protestors. It looked like folks were lining up to be jailed for basic rights. Later, I looked at the images and wondered about the white protestors and demonstrators who fought and bled alongside us. The racial hate obviously didn't cross all color lines, or they wouldn't have been there. They were good people who realized it would take millions of us to rise and beat it back.

After one of the biggest demonstrations we ever had, there were so many prisoners in my hometown that the police had to line everyone up along the street for two miles down the road. The sheer number of protestors alone should have been a clear indication of how angry and tired of it we were. It was said some of the police even tried to incite demonstrators to violence. To be sure, the police did so to try and lock leaders up on a felony charge. Imagine the urge for peaceful protestors being pushed to their limits with spit hawked in their faces along with the N-word. The East Gadsden Brotherhood were ones to stick to their nonviolent approach despite the provocation. They are a fine example of how some of us pushed back without using the same hateful methods of violence and still accomplished change.

Still, accounts of prisoners held in Gadsden Coliseum were terrifying. After being beaten, they were taken to a field full of Klansmen, who teased them about a lynching for a while before they got sent to a thrown-together prison camp. They were half-starved for six days before supporters could find them and finally bail them out. I grew into my teenage years knowing there had been too many close calls, too many near escapes into the bushes while hiding in fear for my people. When could we walk and *all* be called Mister or Miss with dignity? After we secured many of those rights, we now fall into an era where they are often taken for granted, especially by the youth—like those who can sit anywhere they choose on the bus, yet seldom give a thought to how much blood went into that privilege. These kids now eat, live, and are schooled where they formerly spit on us, then burned up what we did establish just to take away our peace at every turn.

We had one of the largest group arrests made during a demonstration anywhere that segregation was being fought at the time. That is just one example of how my hometown of Gadsden and the surrounding state defiantly addressed the racism. I didn't know all of my cousin Robert Avery's heroic journey until I got older and got the full details. Part of it is how at age fifteen he hitchhiked to join Dr. King and the march on Washington. Like the journey of former President Barack Obama, I stand in awe of Robert's journey through the movement as a youth. I asked him to share his own experiences and add another vivid patch to the quilt.

FROM THE EYES OF ROBERT AVERY

"In the summer of '63, there were a lot of demonstrations going on throughout the South. Birmingham had the water hoses and dogs as their weapons, but in Gadsden, the cattle prods were introduced. A lot of events happened throughout the South, but our city became the focal point of the civil rights movement after a white mailman by the name of William Moore was shot and killed about seven miles from downtown. He was on a pilgrimage from Chattanooga, Tennessee, to Jackson, Mississippi, to deliver a letter to Governor Ross Barnett at the time. When he was killed, of course all the civil rights organizations—the Student Non-Violent Coordinating Committee (SNCC), CORE, and the National Association for the Advancement of Colored People (NAACP)—all of them converged on Gadsden because of the killing of this particular postman.

"Here was a white man from Baltimore, Maryland, sitting at home minding his own business but who couldn't stand to see what was happening to black people in the South and decided to do something. He first started talking about walking from Baltimore to Mississippi. Instead, he took the bus to Chattanooga and decided he would take a walk from there to Jackson to protest the things that were happening. He was carrying a sign that was loud and clear on what he was doing, and he had his letter that he was trying to deliver. Before he could, he was shot and killed by a Ku Klux Klansman. They found the shooter and they found the gun, the whole nine yards, but of course, he was never convicted of it.

"That ignited the movement in our city even though we were demonstrating and picketing already; this just heightened everything when all the organizations came to town. Dr. King came [with] a lot of his lieutenants like Hosea Williams and of course Dr. Abernathy, and for these leaders, this city became a priority in the movement at that point. CORE sent in a group of Freedom Walkers because their thing was that they were going to finish delivering that letter to the governor in Mississippi. After they set out to walk in from the spot where the postman had been shot, they were immediately arrested.

"At the height of that summer, one of the major marches had about fifteen hundred people arrested. But not having the capacity to put them in the jails, they took them to a colosseum about two or three miles from downtown. First, they made them all walk in the scorching heat of the summer down a railroad track; it was just unreal what they put them through. So we started doing a lot of picketing and sit-ins at the lunch counters and stores. I was arrested three times in one day, but being a juvenile, they couldn't keep us in jail. That particular day, we were downtown picketing, and they took us down to the courthouse where the judge realized we were juveniles and let us go. We went back downtown, and we were assigned to another store. The police arrested me again. I got reassigned, and I went back down to protest and got arrested a third time. And when they say, 'It takes a village to raise a child,' we were all intertwined there in the '60s during that movement. It's what gave us a lot of power—our tight community.

"I think that knowing why we were doing it was more important than what was happening to us as far as the arresting and everything else. Being a young black growing up during that time, I knew what it was like sitting on the back of the bus or drinking out of the colored-only water fountains or where you couldn't go downtown to sit at a restaurant to eat at a lunch counter. We had to go through the back doors of everything. During that time, I only lived two blocks from the white community, and as young kids, we played with white kids until we got to school age when they started separating us. The school situation was separate but not equal, and I went to a segregated school as a result. You had white and black neighborhoods all over town. It's just that you might have about five or six blocks of blacks and then they were surrounded by a white community. Then you might have ten or twelve blocks of blacks, and then they were surrounded by a white community, and they were on different sides of town. That's just the way it was back when I was growing up because you didn't have those big major areas where there were all black folks.

"By the time of the protests, a lot of our parents, like my mother who was a maid, became afraid of their young children being out there because if they were arrested, they would probably wind up losing their job. There were quite a few folks afraid of it, but my mother wasn't, and she didn't lose her job while some people did. Not a lot of black men were employed because a lot of the employment was made up of domestic workers. That meant the mother was often the breadwinner back in those days. So they had to be extremely careful about their children picketing.

"One thing about it, it was interesting to see that the white females of the household understood and did not give the maids a hard time. It was mostly the white males who were harassing and threatening their jobs while the women of the household often looked the other way. I'm not sure if they didn't want to lose their help or what the case was, but they were not adamant about getting rid of their maids.

"When we first started, probably one or two churches were involved. In fact, when Dr. King came to town, a number of churches didn't want him to speak at theirs. They were afraid that it might get bombed. I remember we were having some issues when the movement first kicked off, but after that, they all came and started participating. You still had a lot of your elderly blacks, who were affluent teachers and people like that who didn't participate in the movement and who stayed away from the demonstrations, mostly because they were afraid of losing their jobs, and I'm sure they were also threatened by the white power structure. All that played heavily on us, particularly knowing that we were fighting for our freedom to do all of those things I mentioned. I think that was the driving force behind a lot of the young people. I know that was the driving force for me anyway. The early part of '63, I was fourteen years old, but I turned fifteen in August. I was an old teen, and my parents pretty much knew I could take care of myself out there protesting.

"Still, the police didn't care whether you were young, old, male or female; they used the cattle prods on everybody. To this day, I have a scar on the inside of my leg where they put it, and it just burned all the way through. Of course, it has to be a powerful shock to get a thousand-pound bull or cow to move the way you want it to move. They were using these to shock people all over their bodies, often their private parts or anywhere else they could stick them. I can remember when they had their first big arrests; there were about six hundred or seven hundred people jailed in one day. When the state troopers came with the cattle prods, they just got white residents off the street and gave them the state trooper shirts. A lot of citizens were out there acting as police officers, and it was very strange. One of the grocery stores in our community was shut down because we could recognize a couple of the sons of the shop owner. They were out there with the deputy sheriff in police shirts with cattle prods. We started boycotting his store, and he had to shut it down.

"It spilled over into the schools, and during the summer of '63 after classes started back, within a couple of weeks, the four young black girls were killed in the bombing of the 16th Street Baptist Church. Us kids would walk out of school and do protesting. It wasn't an everyday thing, but there were times that they picked after school to do some picketing and to protest. It was a spontaneous thing. When you think about four young black girls who were killed in a church of all places and you think about the fact that it could've been you, kids took to the streets. Parents and schoolteachers didn't like it, but there was nothing else they could do about it then. I was fortunate enough to be considered one of the youth leaders. I was allowed to sit in on ad hoc committees that some of the businesspeople in the city wanted to establish to try and get a smooth transition while desegregating the businesses in the downtown. That let me in on the ground floor of that world, to see the changes that were eventually made, such as integrating lunch counters, hiring blacks, and those types of things. I was able to see all of that around the end of that summer when things started to move.

"We all saw tremendous change by the end of that summer and by 1965 a lot more concerning the schools. But there is one thing to 'be free' and have your rights, but it's another thing to be prepared for it, and a lot of us then were not from a financial standpoint. Matter of fact, we were not economically prepared at all. Once they opened the doors and said, 'You can come and have lunch,' we couldn't afford the lunch counters. They said, 'You can stay at any hotel you like,' but we couldn't afford to go stay at the hotels. I saw a need for economic growth and social freedom. I think that sparked me to stay and get involved with government and with business because, again, to have all those freedoms and you can't afford them…you might as well not have them to start with.

"That built my path to try to make things better for me, my children, and eventually my grandchildren. That is what keeps me motivated, and that's what keeps me going now—that and knowing exactly who and what I come from—namely a long line of hard workers. Many of them owned businesses, so I had a lot of inspiration to work and build something important for my people from them. My grandfather was an exception to a lot of things that were happening to black people in the South in his day. He worked for the pipe shop, which was considered good work because they had harder jobs for black folks then. His was called a decent one.

"My father became a tailor by trade. He opened a tailoring shop in downtown Gadsden on a street that was dedicated only to black businesses. He expanded from that later on and bought a couple of cars to put on the taxi line. We didn't grow up dirt poor, but it wasn't affluent like the schoolteachers, the professors, and other professionals. But then there were ten of us in my household, and I think we would be classified as the lower- middle class or right above the poverty line as far as that goes.

"My dad owned his own business alongside other blacks. If you can picture it, we had about six blocks of our major downtown area where all the businesses were located on either side off Broad Street, and then there were streets off there with just a block dedicated to black businesses. My dad's tailoring shop was there, and they had a black restaurant and a black-only theater (except it was owned by white businessmen). It held your other professional blacks also: a dentist, a couple of barber shops—those types of businesses along that strip. It was about two blocks of nothing but black culture. When we were kids, that theater was like our babysitter. When we got out of school, we went down to the shop, and our folks would send us over there until they got done working. I got the chance to see a lot of first- run movies from cowboy pictures to everything else in between. The two white theaters in town you could go to, but you had to sit upstairs. Right after integration, of course the movie theater shut down, and you didn't have a choice; you had to go to the white theater. The white guys that owned the black theater probably owned the other one too. If so, they didn't see the need to own that building when they could just shut it down and put all the black people on the balcony at the other.

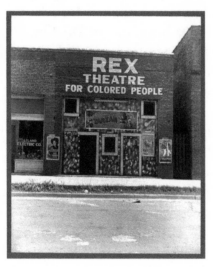

(Example of segregated theater in the South)

"By about 1965 and '66 is when everything finished integrating there, starting with the schools. We got them to start hiring blacks in the stores at some chains. Five or ten of them hired some people—W. T. Grant; Sears is where one of the kids that was active in the movement with us got hired after graduation. In fact, he started a career there and ended up managing several stores throughout the South. We had to force the issue though—that is what was in the agreement: to stop the demonstrations and the picketing if they started opening the doors. We didn't have to do a lot of demonstrations after '63 and after we came to that agreement.

"Once we filed a lawsuit to desegregate everything, the courts agreed with us after we sat there and worked it out.

After that, the schools were integrated by '64, the first year that all the blacks in our town went to an all- white high school. It was lawyers out of Birmingham like J. Mason Davis, a big civil rights attorney back in those days who represented Dr. King and some of the lawsuits in Birmingham. Men like Oscar Adams, who was the first black to serve on the Alabama Supreme Court; he was a civil rights attorney also along with Fred Gray, who did some work on it too. He was well-known all over the country as being one of Dr. King's attorneys, but he did some things here in Gadsden during that time as well. Also, U. W. Clement, who also came along during that time, who had just retired as a federal judge.

"All of them I mentioned came on later to integrate the steel plant and file lawsuits at Goodyear and those major industries here. Before the integration of the plants, a lot of the blacks were just in the janitorial service there. Some industries such as Goodyear had what they call a Rubber Gang where these guys would open rubber out of the box carts. They stood out, but usually they had designated jobs for the blacks at both places. They couldn't build tires because I don't think the first blacks started in that until around 1970 or maybe '71, and those were the money-making jobs. Goodyear and the steel plant offered work that kept this community afloat. If you worked at either one of those, even if you were a janitor, then those were the upper-class black people. Even the janitors there were making just as much as schoolteachers were during that time. That's why it was hard to put my family into a class; we owned businesses, but those other positions offered the affluence. Eventually, the steel plants shut down, but Goodyear is still here and still the major employer. Now we've been able to diversify, adding a lot of poultry plants that service the fast-food industry. The major automobile industry has picked up tremendously in this area also. The Honda plant is only about twenty miles from Gadsden, and a lot of the people worked there or in one of their local service plants.

"Economically, things are about the same as when we protested for change. The only problem is now blacks are still underemployed in this community, and we have high unemployment with our youth. There are things that can be done to change that, but the powers that be, from a political standpoint, don't want to do that. Even so, we're in the process of working some things out. We just gained a majority of the city council, which was, up until three years ago, a majority white council. It was hard to get things done or bring in businesses because many of the people at the top wanted to keep things the way they were. They wanted to be the big fish in the little pond still, and they didn't want to expand the pond. Now we've got a majority black council and looking at expanding. I feel good about the future of the community and the things that can be done to impact our young people. It's been hard to crack that network, but we're slowly bringing it down.

"Next year (2018) is another election, and I'm almost certain we'll wind up with a black mayor, which means that will have put not only a crack in the dike—it would have busted the dike wide open. Up until 1986, the city was run by three white men. We had a mayor and two commissioners; we didn't even have a city council. The three commissioners were elected at large, and the mayor was elected at large. We also had a public safety commissioner and a public works commissioner. In '85, we filed a lawsuit to change that form of government to a mayor-council form because black people couldn't be equally represented or even fairly represented otherwise. We went to a mayor-council form of government in 1986, now with a mayor and seven council members and a majority black council.

"In '86 when we filed a lawsuit, I was one of the ones to help it, and the reason I was able to do that was that I had run for public office before that. To show that we had been harmed, we needed to show someone who ran but couldn't win because of the at-large elections. That is how we were able to change the elections. One of the things that we were able to do was draw the district lines. Being a lifelong resident here, I drew them myself, and some of the older guys who were involved in the lawsuit—in the NAACP and Voters League—those groups wanted to go to a five-member council and a mayor. I told them that wouldn't be good because during that time, we could only get one black district and maybe an influence district, and I tried to tell them that if we went to a seven-member council, we would almost be guaranteed two black districts and hopefully one influence district.

"They kept arguing with me and telling me I couldn't do it, yet in the end, I finally convinced everyone. We were not just able to draw seven districts, we were able to get two black candidates elected in 1986. I was the first black candidate to get elected because I didn't have a runoff in my race; the other black had a runoff and won his. Two black officials elected in 1986 up until 2008 when there was a third added. In 2012, we got our fourth black official elected. We just put our third black business in our local mall, and over these years, I got to watch and be a part of all of this progress.

"Now that I'm off the council after I had served for twenty-four years, I consult all over the country in about fifteen different states. One thing I advise to young and old is about small business ownership and fighting any systems that try to stop that. It goes beyond homeownership and into business because our young people need something to grab hold of economically.

"My grandparents owned property and homes—several of them. Some of my mother's brothers owned property. On the Knowles side, all of them probably, except for my mother and one of her brothers, owned their homes, and Mathew still owns some property here in Gadsden. But we also held some position of ownership in businesses and in homes before those integration changes. Of course, those changes for our freedom were worth it, except for the fact that now, the whole block except for one business is a city parking lot.

"To destroy people's heritage, you have to destroy their landmarks—those places you can go back and point to and say, 'My dad owned a business there, and Mr. Joe owned a business there,' or even 'I went to school there' because they tore down a lot of black schools. For example, Gadsden City High School replaced the three former city high schools in 2006 to 2007.

"That's the way you destroy a heritage and the way you destroy the culture of people when you don't have anything that you can point to and say it was ours. That influences black youth. Many don't think about home ownership or about business ownership. Not when we can't go back and point to something our parents or our people owned—not when they are busy tearing everything down."

Interlude

NOCCALULA'S RISE

This interlude is part love story gone sour and part town ghost story as a result. Yet for me, it explains a lot about life growing up in Gadsden and my adolescent rebellion during that time. For me, the stories behind Noccalula Falls and Lookout Mountain, as well as what happened to the people there, all foreshadow the defiance of my hometown in the '60s and give history to the spirit that watered it.

First, I'll give my brief backstory and connection to both places and how they later led me to a deeper understanding of myself and my hometown. In 2017, I revisited the famous Noccalula Falls and walked the grounds where I once worked for two years as a grounds caretaker at ages sixteen and seventeen. I always kept a job somewhere when I was a kid. Inspired by my parents' and grandparents' entrepreneurial spirits, I liked money coming in. I started with my own business at age nine, buying candy from the store near the school and reselling it to my classmates at St. Martin de Porres (until the nuns shut me down). I later worked at the Goodyear plant, and I kept various jobs during the summer. I got lucrative positions, mainly because of what I had accomplished on the basketball team.

By the time I was sixteen years old, I was even making a name for myself in the sports sections of the newspaper from junior high up through my senior year. Due to such status, I became a lifeguard at the recreation center during the summer. It is ironic we weren't invited to swim there, but a tall, black lifeguard was on duty protecting those who could. This new position afforded me many notes slipped my way from girls who went to my school.

Hiiiiii Mathew! Can you meet me after school? one would usually say. These notes led to secret rendezvous up on Lookout Mountain, our local lovers' lane. What would make me defy tradition? Nobody in my family or community that I knew of had openly dated white people. Not to mention the fact that to marry one would have been illegal in Alabama at that time anyway. What would make me grow bold enough to step over the line drawn by law and popular opinion?

My mother would say stuff like "Don't bring no nappy-headed black girl up in here!" But that didn't mean I was to bring home a white one. I knew what she meant. The brainwashing of the slave owners held fast with rural folks and many others of her generation. They carried the wishes of slave owners who favored the biracial traits they could produce over authentically powerful African or Native American ones that stood out. These unsuspecting old folks passed down the desires of racists in the form of colorism. Although people, like my mother, who thought along this line weren't aware of it, what they felt was common, even if not spoken out loud, leading all the way up to the brown paper bag standards that I met later in college at Fisk, where I experienced this form of racism—colorism—in my community.

These standards left me with few social options that summer, especially after being chased and threatened with a beating from the kids calling me "Oreo." I knew not to date any girls from Carver, so I wore my orange and black jacket through a sea of white girls who began to notice me. I also noticed them. I was no better able to ignore puberty than I was my mother's orders to integrate those white schools. At that stage, my hormones saw no color lines, and apparently neither did theirs. My need for companionship saw no barriers, and few of them offered up any.

I had probably been arrested by some of these girls' kinfolks during the marches, but they were there batting eyes and making it clear—I could go there. I got bold enough to have kissed one on the front of the school steps and landed in trouble in the vice-principal's office. That was the beginning of me finding myself in somebody's office or before a red-faced, angry administrator for getting caught crossing that line. It seems amazing to me now that Emmett Till's murder for allegedly making a pass at a white girl in the summer of '55 was just thirteen years before the summer I dated a few. What was I doing? This was in a state that didn't get rid of laws banning interracial marriage until the year 2000. Alabama held on despite the infamous civil rights Supreme Court decision in *Virginia v. Loving*, the case that finally allowed interracial marriage.

Alabama was a state where somebody could snatch you up out of that parked car on Lookout Mountain overlooking all those disapproving white folks below fornicating with one of their teenagers and quite easily lynch you. They could at least arrest and punish you for daring the crime. It was 1968 that first summer of risks, the same year some racist killed Dr. King. There I was, foolish (or daring) enough to climb a hill and break a social taboo after leaving work at Noccalula Falls.

The impulsive risk-taking. The defiance. I wondered where it came from first. I could blame some influence on my parents, who dared to do what they wanted without asking. In truth, they mostly did their best to keep me out of risky situations like all good parents. So where else did the influences come from, I ask? In 1968, you could come up missing or a splattered headline across some Alabama newspaper: "The strangest and stupidest fruit killed for courting a white girl," it would say. People did it all the time, but it was dangerous and kept down low if possible.

I think I discovered a clue the summer when I was working at Noccalula Falls. However, it didn't form a complete picture until almost fifty years later when I went back again. I worked as a custodian of the park grounds with just one other man, an old white guy who would mostly go off and get drunk. This position left me all alone on that 250-acre public park—closing as late as midnight. On some days, the mist from the waterfall would rise and steam up the falls that ran concurrently with the town's water supply.

It was a pretty picture during the day where tourists would point and say they could see the spirit of the park's namesake in the mists. Southerners do love their ghost stories. As one of only two people to clean up and close at night, that made it downright spooky. There are some dark and heavily wooded areas in that park. Down those roads are these old log-cabin-style buildings holding concessions and things like replicas of the "old post office," etc. Some look like they snatched them off an old cotton plantation from the 1800s. They took on a creepy effect after dark, sitting on either side of a railroad track that ran a tourist train around the park. After midnight, I saw every kind of animal you could name out there in the woods crossing those tracks. I heard every screech, howl, and moan that a creature could make from deer to bears to whatever else was out there with that old drunk and me every night.

Hanging behind all that was the legend of the falls that you could run into at every turn. The year I began working there, the city started the work on a statue and plaque, which by my last year there in 1969 was put near the entrance. It tells the story of Noccalula, a doomed Cherokee princess. Before that, I don't think we kids—black or white—got any *real* Native American history in school. But the Gadsden area has a special connection to the Native people in far too many ways to separate in this quilt: the street I grew up on, Tuscaloosa Avenue, the county named Etowah, and even in one interpretation, "Alabama" is Choctaw for "Here we rest." That would be far from the truth for those who, once white settlers arrived, got *no* rest.

Here I give some of my backstories, but I will also share those of Native people who, for all I know based on family stories, could have been some of my own. Either way, they were another group, like ours, that fought white oppression hundreds of years before Lingo and Wallace's brand of hate ever arrived in Gadsden. With both stories, you will see how the two groups share similar themes, both ending up with the same spirit of defiance.

I'm sure the first white settlers immediately recognized the natural beauty of that area. Anybody can still drive through, look at the trees, the green hillsides, the lakes, and see the same tempting views they did. After all that war and migration, the white settlers were ready for some rest too— never mind on fully occupied land. Maybe they also heard the rumor that the waterfall in Gadsden had nearby mineral springs with healing effects. Why not stay and get some then?

By the time I worked there, the legend behind Noccalula Falls was already in place. Stories about deaths of Native

Americans were popular newspaper fillers after the civil war. It's not surprising Centre Alabama's *The Cherokee Advertiser* printed the story of Noccalula way back in 1867. There are so many versions of suicidal and heartbroken Native princesses in the South that even Mark Twain wrote jokingly about it. *The Gadsden Times* of May 7, 1895, published its version, said to have been gathered from old families and holdouts from the Indian removals in the 1830s. That story gave us what became our town's official name for Black Creek Falls— "Noccalula" —when it first opened in 1946.

With pennies collected by the Gadsden Women's Club from school kids, among other donations, they had a famous Belgian-born baroness to sculpt a tribute. She selected a local fifteen-year-old girl from Glencoe high school as the "perfect reincarnation" of the fallen princess. Stereotypical costumes, wig, and even a chance for Gadsden's citizens to get an autograph from "the real Noccalula" followed. I don't know the numbers of the remaining population of Cherokees, Creeks, Choctaws, and other Native tribes at that time, but I wonder if there were any available as models for the statue and if so why none were used.

By the time I left after my last summer there in September of 1969, it was a tourist attraction with a nine-foot bronze image of a defiant leap in progress. Her story gave a sad and eerie quality to those mists and to the sounds I heard closing the place each night. If the legend is true, it would add an ironic twist to the Gadsden piece of my story. Just being told the story was enough to influence a young mind working under the shadow of that legend every night when the sun went down.

We always heard Noccalula was the daughter of a prominent chief, living in a village within sight of a great waterfall during the late 1700s and early 1800s. Our own Black Creek Falls, as it was called back in its early days, already had a village of Cherokees living near it, so they used that to pinpoint the location. No story about a princess is complete without talk of her great beauty or a whole bunch of young men waiting in line to marry her. The legend says her father wanted her to wed a chief from another tribe—a move that would bring formerly warring tribes together and peace to the whole region. Apparently, Noccalula had other ideas. She was head over heels with a young brave from her tribe. "No deal," said her daddy. "...It's my way or, for him, the highway." Not only did he forbid the marriage, but he also ran the brave she loved right up out of the whole region. On her wedding day, dressed to the nines and facing a marriage into a clan that was not her choice, Noccalula said, "Hell no." She quietly slipped away from the feast, ran to the rock that hangs over the falls, and then dove to her death in grief and defiance.

It was *her* way or no way, peace between clans be damned. She drowned in the water, and I always imagined it was with a face full of tears. Because nobody wants to die when life could hold so much potential—first love, friendships, doing whatever you like with no parental limitation. But when offered a miserable, controlled life under somebody's hateful thumb, you might just choose "Give me liberty or give me death" too.

Noccalula slipped away forever off the rocks of those falls but not really. The devastated chief named both the waterfall and the surrounding gorge in memory of her. The plaque and statue are there to tell the tourists she lived. Noccalula and other tribes' marks remain there in other significant ways too, just above it, high on a hill overlooking the town. Just a short and twisted, uphill drive from the falls takes you to Lookout Mountain, the foothills of the Appalachian Mountains, with the best views for miles. It was the spot where two people—forbidden by law in the state to marry—could be hormonal teenagers. The cement patch where I would park with my forbidden friends I now find covered in colorful graffiti. New generations of young lovers no doubt still go there because it was a prime spot for some reason. No police or parents would come up there and bother us, although I'd bet neither would approve. Still, nobody rattled our windows or chased us off to jail.

Just below us, the misty falls got fed by rainwater running off a ninety-foot drop into the Black Creek Gorge. Thousands of years of water running off Lookout Mountain into that ravine is what carved the tourist attraction where I worked by day. By night, I must have felt some secret power up there with that view, parked above the whole town, breaking white men's rule number one. Almost fifty years later, armed with more research and understanding, it all fit together in the combined histories of many people's defiance. For example, that spot where we parked had its own powerful backstory.

Lookout Mountain, right near where we sat in parked cars in secret, is where the braves fought the Last Battle of the Cherokees during the eighteenth-century Nickajack Expedition. It was also the spot of the 1863 Battle of Lookout Mountain during the American Civil War. For perspective, my great-grandfather Pinkney Moore would have been just ten years old, born about 1853 when that took place. These battles weren't just some textbook incidents our schools may or may not have taught us; they were a part of my family's current affairs back when it happened.

Two generations later on that Native American battleground, as a teenager, I was essentially breaking not just a cultural taboo but a barrier in myself. Everything leading up to my life at that age, especially that bloody summer of 1963 when black people stood up and fought back, was all about breaking some door down. This bit of defiance on my part wasn't some noble cause on behalf of my community; it was simply for me. As a teenager, I had no clue the history I sat upon or the battleground blood that mixed with the falling rainwater down into the gorge. I imagine now, it made it special. In fact, the water in our region was swimming with stories, like Hokes Bluff, a small part of the Gadsden metropolitan area. It was a lookout station for Native American tribes, who could see over great distances up, down, and across the Coosa River from there. That was also where the Cherokee Natives were gathered together to be sent on to Gunter's Landing (now Guntersville), and then on west to Oklahoma on the Trail of Tears. This town has its own legend with Tawannah Springs, named for another Native American princess by that name. It's said she grieved herself to death after her cousin—Princess Noccalula—jumped from the falls in Gadsden.

Between the river of tears and blood from the ousted Natives and the anger and grief of denied lovers soaking the springs and falls that helped stir our table water, I had an idea Gadsden was hardened for a reason. Soon after the time my maternal great-great grandfather, Calvin Moore, was born, during the 1820s and 1830s, both tribes and all other southeastern Native people were pushed to Indian Territory in what is now Oklahoma.

The legend in my own family was that Dave Hogue was part Cherokee. It played on my mind back then as it would any young person struggling with their racial identity in the '50s and '60s. Maybe our people needed to hear they had some warrior in their blood. The slave owners had stripped away African history and any original language from families as if it were a bad dream. What was left of Africa, few of our elders talked about what they remembered. That left them to use the Native American tribes to answer the question of where the long hair, high cheekbones, or light skin came from in a relative—anything but "rape by Massa" made those looks exotic and not so shameful. Hell, even white people claim to be "part Indian." The braves and how hard they fought for their freedom are things even white settlers must have admired. None of them brag about being three-quarter Negro by blood; that's why I suspect that.

The Cherokee and Creeks who surrounded the slaves, as well as the freed slaves, all faced the same oppressor—white men. I know Professor Skippy Gate's research states very few tribes intermixed with those African descendants, but it stands against many a family legend that says otherwise. Those "my folks were Indian" stories are as persistent as Noccalula's legend. A belief *that* strong will breathe a myth into life.

Once the warriors and braves met men like Andrew Jackson with his fierce hatred, they were removed. They lost after many long battles and that other weapon white settlers carried—the biological H-bombs they put on the Natives' immune systems. Had the many tribes not gotten sick, how different might history be? That left all the breathtaking views and greens of the Coosa River Valley and all the surrounding Southeast available for white settlers. The cotton revolution drew in profits, and Alabama Fever migrators poured in.

Two years before my great-grandmother Rosetta (Moore) Hogue was born, the last forced removal east of the Mississippi of the Cherokee took place in 1838. Because they found gold near Dahlonega, Georgia, bringing on the Georgia Gold Rush, they needed the elbow room. Between two thousand and six thousand of nearly seventeen thousand Native Americans who were forcibly removed died en route. I'm sure once white settlers took in the views from Lookout Mountain, they were hell-bent on having it for themselves. There were other tribes in those areas as well. Chickasaw Nation in Oklahoma still recognizes No. 79 as part of its former land, which is a small portion of where that tribe was. After the No. 79 Treaty, there were almost no Natives remaining in the area after 1816. The exception was any intermarried couples or ones choosing to stay as US citizens.

That means there were still some Native Americans left in the area who looked like the woman pictured here. Apparently, there weren't enough to select one to model for Noccalula's statue, unless the story was that the young, white, blue-eyed Glencoe, Alabama, model was some degree of Native. If so, it wasn't mentioned.
(Choctaw Belle by Phillip Romer, via Wikimedia Commons)

If you ever walk the grounds there now, you will have a few backstories to run together. There are the Native Americans who defied the order to march their way to Oklahoma, battling atop our future lovers' lane instead. There is a princess defying her father's wish to bring peace through an unhappy marriage and dying with suppressed desires for whom she wanted to love. Then hundreds of years later, a young black teen with a cattle-prod burn on an arm now wrapped around the neck of a white girl carries out an unconscious protest to his own repressions of choice. He was a teenager who was defying the law and his community to selfishly free his young desires because why not? Gadsden itself was defiant.

The year 1963 was just when it came to a head for the world to see. It had been a simmering pot for self-determination and a "my way or no way" mindset for ages. The waters soaking it run through Black Creek Gorge, past old Civil War carvings and secret caves and forts built by Native Americans and their battlegrounds, intermingling with the table water of blacks and whites alike. In other words, I think we were all bred on the waters of defiance and didn't even know it.

PART III

UNIVERSITY LESSONS IN RACE

UT CHATTANOOGA–BOUND

From 1963 and into my high school years, I internalized much of what I'd experienced, and it was slowly building up by my senior year. It would soon be time to choose a college, and that could mean my escape from that town. My ideal choice was the University of Denver, but if I had a second choice, I was fine with UT Chattanooga because the campus was so nice, and I compared their twelve thousand students against the seven hundred or so the junior college in Gadsden would offer. Also, it was one of the top universities in the country with an excellent basketball program; it was like comparing a Volkswagen to a Rolls-Royce for me. As a ballplayer, when you're young like that, you think in your head about playing in the NBA. When you play at a junior college, you must go from there to a four-year college first. That made my choice to leave easier by far, and I was already planning that faraway college life to escape that whole scene by the time I was sixteen.

Senior year, when it came time for me to choose where to go, my mother's own choice was set: "You're not going outside the state." She thought the University of Denver was too far. Her eyes were on Gadsden's local junior college, and while the campus was pretty, I'd had enough of all things local. As inspiring as they were, at that age, that sadly included my parents' influence. UT Chattanooga was a close enough compromise, so I forced the issue, and my mother bent because it was at least closer to home. There, once again, I was one of the first blacks among about forty students to enter the University of Tennessee at Chattanooga—in a sea of twelve thousand white students. It didn't take me long to get to the city and find a place to call my "spot" down on 9th Street. You didn't see any white folks there because it was where all the black restaurants and clubs were concentrated. Of course, they also had a white section of town, but I never bothered memorizing the name because I just knew not to go over there.

It was special for me coming in as a basketball star because back then, they gave you a little scholarship pocket money to get adjusted. It wasn't a fortune, but it supplemented the money I made the first two summers I still worked back in Gadsden. I had enough to drive a nice Oldsmobile, and I bought new clothes to hang out looking the part. The big deal at that time was the movie and soundtrack *Superfly*, and it played out in my head when I bought that green lounge jacket with yellow fur, the tan turtleneck, and the brown pants—so I could go from small-town kid to superfly myself. At that time, I wasn't frequently communicating with my parents. Seldom did I talk to them when I left home, especially my dad, because it was like when I was a child growing up—he was always working. I rarely went back to Gadsden after I left for college besides working those summers between my freshman and sophomore year at the Goodyear plant. My childhood memories of Gadsden left me with despair and the tale of two cities.

By the time I was nineteen, I was becoming my own man. Once I left home that last summer, my mom never got involved in school anymore, and Dad just wasn't that kind anyway. They were both amazing, inspiring parents in so many ways, but by the time I left home, I was in turmoil over my need to be independent. I felt the same as most black people at that time in America—wanting complete freedom and not under somebody's thumb, even one attached to your own parent's hand.

How else do you test-fly your adulthood from under the wings of another adult? If they resist your need for independence and self-control, you will rebel or just walk away. Every guardian eventually faces that reality. So did Uncle Sam. The 1960s and '70s were all about a specific flavor of freedom for American adolescents who believed independence meant being completely self-determining. "When do we get to be the adults in the room?" our generation asked. It was like those "terrible twos" all over again when you become a teenager trying to test the perimeters of how much power you have. In your young adulthood, you wonder what sort of authority you can claim. Eventually, it is a power you need to test outside of the house.

Maybe I became a master salesman just from learning how to negotiate my own choices around a "my way or no way" mother, one who didn't let anyone play into her decisions. I sharpened my horns on one of the toughest women in town. But that racial environment was no place to continue exerting my manhood—not with my ideas about how it should be lived.

Away at college, I had time to think about my parents' roles differently. To draw a necessary line between being a good son and a grown man, I had to be brutally honest about what I lacked at home besides freedom. You can inspire your child by being great yourself, but sometimes they also need you to hand them some tools. Although a great craftsman, my dad left certain areas of me uncarved. The distance college gave allowed me time and space to work on those issues.

For example, my dad never taught me how to shave or ever had a conversation about sex with me. I had to learn that stuff on my own and often in disastrous ways. My mom never had a conversation about sex or puberty either, except to voice her preference for a certain type of girl for me. I thought about it: What young man doesn't at heart want to please his mother? In high school and college, I started aiming only for very fair-complexioned girls for that reason and secretly dated what I had better access to—the white girls whom I met in private. My folks never knew or said anything about them if they did, although in that era none of them would have approved, I'm sure. My exposure to white cheerleaders, and later those campus girls who had experience and more freedom, made my coming-of-age one steeped in both sexual and racial conflicts. It was better not played out under my parents' noses back home. It was still against a backdrop of small Southern towns with Confederate flags waving at the schools where we played games for UT Chattanooga. Unbeknownst to them, I was a big attraction for the young women, even while they were busy name-calling during the games.

I came to think of places like those as ones where you're going to experience that. On the other hand, I had to adjust to these subtle forms of prejudice and envy. In the classroom, because of my sports privileges (even though I was still black), the white students would be jealous, and it showed. Here we black athletes had scholarships and all these perks, and some of them had come from even less, and it brought out a lot of envy. It was a strange feeling, a white person envying me. It was still all subtle mistreatment because I was different. For me, racism, colorism, sexism, and any other forms of discrimination are cut from the same mean cloth. Hatred might wear a lot of different names, but underneath it boils down to the same effects.

Between my freshman and sophomore year, I worked back in Gadsden and chose December to stay on campus. Four of us black teammates remained in our athletic dorm over the holidays while all the other students went home. Guys will be guys, and every so often, you'd have a girl in your room when some other guy, being silly, would knock on the door. When I got a knock over the Christmas break, I thought it was another one of the guys who also stayed.

I had a girl in there who was puffing on a cigarette, so the room was all smoky. I thought it was one of the guys, so I got up and yelled at him before I even responded, "Ralph, get away from my door!" It was a minute or two before I even opened it because I was sure it was him. That's why I finally answered in just my underwear. When I opened it, however, it was another red-faced man catching me in a taboo. This time, it was my coach. It wasn't so smoky that he couldn't see the white girl on the bed. He looked at me all angry and yelled, "If I were you, I'd get her out of here *right now!*" I did so quickly, and I thought that might be the end of it—until I got called into his office later. He told me the school had a thing called "social probation."

"You know I could put you on that, which would mean you couldn't play basketball anywhere for two years, but I'm not going to do that. Just know at the end of this season you will not be at the University of Chattanooga. You can bet on it. So, start looking for a place to go to school," he said.

This is what I think. I can't say I know this as fact; it's just what I feel about that situation. My roommate, who was a white player, told on me because he and I were competing for the same position on the basketball team. No other time did the coach come and knock on my door in that way. He had to be tipped off, and that is who would have done it.

One thing about it—the coach was hard on everyone. It was the year that I left when they fired him. There are several types of coaches: Those who scream when you don't win a game and at every mistake you make. Then they take you out of the game or threaten to, so then you can't relax and play well. Other coaches let you play and work through your mistakes and try to get your nerves down. The coach who caught me was that screamer kind of guy.

He is the one who gave me a nickname that stuck with me all through college—"Snake." It happened during halftime, which is when the coach would tell us what we were doing wrong. He said I was acting like I was playing defense, but I wasn't really doing it. "You're like all down, looking like you're going to prance on somebody just like a damn snake!"

he yelled. After every game, all the black players would go and drink beer down on 9th Street, and that night we hung out and laughed about it, and that's when it stuck. I was cool with it because all of us had nicknames. I finally had one too, and it wasn't a big deal. That's the kind of coach he was though, that kind of mean. We had a good record despite that pressure. Sophomore year after Christmas, knowing that the coach was going to put me out of school for catching me like that, I didn't play in any game. Only when we played Tennessee State, the black university, did he put me in, and we almost beat them. He wanted to win at all costs—especially against a black school. They had a player who became a star NBA player, and he helped them have an incredible record. Beating him would have been a big deal in the coach's eyes, even if it meant putting in that white-girl-dating "Snake" in his eyes. We lost by two points, and deep inside I was happy we lost.

Ironically, we had scrimmages at Fisk University at one point. It was interesting that a white school would only do that with black ones that were so bad they knew they were going to beat the heck out of them, and so it would be a good scrimmage. I did well playing against them, and afterward, the Fisk coach came and whispered in my ear, "If you ever need a school, call me…" Dangerous risks. That's how I got to Fisk.

1. Willie Walker
2. Leon Rucker
3. Charles Campbell
4. Steve Richardson
5. Bruce Mitchell
6. James Cheeks
7. Robert Williams
8. Joel Hobbs
9. Mathew Knowden
10. Robert Jordan
11. Clarence Howard
12. Albert Woodard
13. Kenneth Parks
14. Gustar Williams
15. Larry Ford
16. Jerry Hauser
17. David Stuckey
Not Pictured:
Dewitt Bowden
Kenneth Paris
Vernon Porter

FISK OUT OF WATER

Since I was forced out of my predominantly white college, I had no choice but to pack up the following year and become a fish out of water with my own people at Fisk. It's a fascinating historically black college, and as an educator, I encourage everyone to research the long histories behind all Historically Black Colleges and Universities (HBCUs). Here's an interesting note on Fisk from their website: "The school was named in honor of General Clinton B. Fisk of the Tennessee Freedmen's Bureau, who provided the new institution with facilities in former Union Army barracks near the present site of Nashville's Union Station. In these facilities, Fisk convened its first classes on January 9, 1866." In 1866, Nashville got the Fisk Free Colored School with the help of the American Missionary Association and donations by several abolitionists. Designed to educate former slaves and freedmen, once that type of support dried up, the school struggled to stay afloat. Enter music, which saved the day for me in many ways during my Fisk years and later in life. It alone kept their doors open way back then.

Their music director was a missionary who thought of fundraising by utilizing their young black vocalists singing old spirituals that echoed the slave era, which those first singers would have known well. Each of the nine was a former slave who made up the Fisk Jubilee Singers. By touring to raise money for the school, these talents got little love from segregated establishments, whether restaurants or hotels. Eventually, the group would become well known and even continues to perform with a new generation of talent. Just think of the fate of the school resting on the musical backs of nine former slaves. In fact, once the original members disbanded, one of the singers complained of ill health as result of the poor treatment they received while touring and it having a grueling and emotional effect on them.

I had never had that black experience or its rich history before in school, and it was fascinating. Fisk has always produced notable alumni who have made a significant impact in areas of art, music, and government: WEB Dubois, Nikki Giovani, Congressman John Lewis, Hazel O'Leary, James Weldon Johnson, Marion Berry, and Judith Jamison, just to name a few. At the majority-white schools I attended, why would they bother to give such narrow student demographics any specific black history at all? Not at any of those schools I integrated did I get that cultural enrichment. However, Fisk was an all-black historic university, and it was just the reverse

—no white students whatsoever—with plenty of access to our history and culture if you wanted it. Now there were a lot of students who looked white honestly, and that was interesting to experience too—the skin-color thing. Fisk was so dramatically different in that you had a majority of darker-complexioned students in the student body at Tennessee State, whereas a large percent of Fisk's students were lighter skinned. If you were of darker complexion, you were likely an athlete. One famous professional ballplayer's daughter attended, and because she was a darker skin tone, I remember some students saying, "Oh yeah, her dad gave a million dollars to the school so she could get in." That was how I experienced that fine line at Fisk.

When I initially got to Nashville, I literally spent as much time at Tennessee State as I did at Fisk because I felt more comfortable over there. It was because the economic climate was more of what I was used to. I was isolated in that Fisk atmosphere coming from my background, where the kids were from higher-income black families. Many of their parents were wealthy entrepreneurs, doctors, and attorneys, and we had some international presence from the Bahamas as well.

Just seeing these guys driving fancy cars—and they were in college—with these beautiful ladies, them changing clothes three times a day—that was all new to me. When I first got there, I was somewhat a loner because I didn't know even one person at that point (other than the coach who invited me to Fisk). I didn't spend that much time with the basketball players because they were just the opposite of me. Most of them were from Nashville, not all but most, and they came from a tough life. They lived off campus, and so there wasn't that synergy. Fortunately, my fraternity, Omega Psi Phi, helped me through that transition. I don't know how it would have been otherwise because I had few social options. I pledged in 1972, and we were the second line to ever go over at UT Chattanooga. There again, I found myself as one of the first through the door somewhere, and there was altogether eight of us. It's a fraternity, so you take in any of the members like a brother regardless of whether or not you've ever seen them before in your life. That brotherhood was there for me at both UTC and Fisk. UTC had all the major fraternities, but it was segregated, so ours did nothing with them, and they did nothing with us. They had frat houses that they lived in, and of course, we didn't have even one, especially being new on the campus. We just had our meetings and our parties and did our thing by ourselves.

There were Vanderbilt, Tennessee State, and Fisk as the three major schools in Nashville. But there were another ten smaller universities and colleges in its surrounding area. This led to a college community that was overall larger and more diverse than I expected. I saw open interracial dating, hippies, Black Panthers—you name it, the quad might have them all congregating at once under the blare of music. Besides my fraternity brothers, I had few social options but many opportunities to mingle with music. It was the start of the 1970s when I got to Nashville. It was a period of transition for both America and me. It was also one of the most energetic and thriving eras where music became the anthem of our movement.

You know, the soundtrack to your life can help you pinpoint not just where you were but what you might have been feeling or doing when a song was out. You could forget the year but remember Marvin Gaye was singing "What's Going On?" and remember everything else, including the scent of the person you were dancing with. That is what those Fisk years and, in fact, these memories have underneath them—a powerful soundtrack. We needed that music to keep us sane, and it did. Over time, I would not only embrace my Fisk experience but appreciate it. While the racists were trying to beat our heads in, the Temptations, O'Jays, and the Spinners were getting us to nod them to a beat. They were in heavy rotation down on 9th Street where we heard them most. Back then, you didn't listen to music on your mobile phone because we didn't have them or an iPad. We only listened to music at home and when in a car, but seldom were we in our cars. Sitting in a dormitory room trying to listen to your choice of music also provided a challenge.

At UT Chattanooga, I had a white roommate, so we agreed that we just wouldn't play music when the other one was in the room. He liked country, and I didn't; I liked R&B, and he didn't. So seldom did I listen to music other than when I went down to 9th Street during my UT Chattanooga years.

When I got to Nashville, it was as if music was everywhere at once in my life, and I listened to and even hung out with some of the greats. There was this area called Elysian Fields in Nashville where I got exposed to Lonny Liston Smith and Grover Washington and all these amazing jazz musicians. When Lonnie Liston Smith came to Nashville, I had a party for him at my apartment because I had a nice place there. That is what kept me busy when I wasn't into anything else—music. Interesting side note: Oprah Winfrey also later lived in the apartment complex where I stayed in Nashville. She went to Tennessee State while I attended Fisk. I occasionally ran into her back then and even went to her dad's barbershop a few times while I lived there.

It was a stimulating atmosphere full of bright minds with tons of potential, a thriving time for young people. Marvin Gaye was hot, Chaka Khan, the Ohio Players, Curtis Mayfield—that's what I was into, back when it was a meaningful time in black music. For a college kid discovering the world, these musical voices were ambassadors to the one I would enter later. Music was something that woke up all the other experiences around me. In placing the details of those years by using music as the map, it also brought out the colors, flavors, and highlights of college life and my memories of all my earlier flirtations in music as well. I loved music. My family had helped make it an escape from a hard life, and it was the foundation of black households in the 1960s and 1970s.

It was our protest anthem when we needed it in every form, and even when it got raunchy, it was because we now could say what was on our minds. We started using music to say what was real once we, the protesting youth movement, turned into adults. Those songs like "Ball of Confusion" and "Say It Loud," James Brown's hit telling us to be black and proud, spoke volumes about our mindsets. Knowing what music meant to me as a social connector, I gravitated toward the arts in the early-70s. Meeting musicians like Roy Ayers and others who would come through performing, and being backstage with them, opened the pathway for my later involvement in that world.

In college, it was all about using music for helping me get past the pressure and any fears. Sundays and the weekends were when I would always go to the park and listen to jazz. Out there, I saw everything from guys in dashikis to ones in platform shoes smoking pot. There were plenty of afros and afro picks in back pockets. It was so much to offer that I had never seen before, and I just explored it all. I didn't just stay on the Fisk campus; I went over to Tennessee State and the Vanderbilt area because they had a vibrant place called Hadley Park. These parks were where the whole energy was on the weekends.

I saw a live show that only costed fifty cents with Earth, Wind & Fire back when they had a female lead vocalist, Jessica Cleaves, singing my favorite song at the time, "Think About Loving You." I got to know these groups by going backstage or to an after-party; I was fascinated by that whole crowd. It was at this point when I first met my frat brother

David Lombard, who was then GM of the Fisk FM radio show. We used to sit and talk about one day being in the music industry and starting girl groups. Years later, he put together En Vogue, and I put together Destiny's Child. That fact always amazes me.

While the colorism and racism both on campus and in the country were spinning out, there I was spinning toward music that not only saved me but was my destiny. Meanwhile, there were world headlines: Watergate. Vietnam. Cold War. Space Race. That would sum up America's preoccupation during my early college years in the 1970s. Instead of bobbing my head up and down in my fur-trimmed turtleneck in the quad or hanging out with famous musicians at after-parties, I could have been carrying a gun and a canteen in a jungle for Uncle Sam. I was fortunate two things happened. One is the draft lottery, where we had a specific number associated with our birthday. If yours fell on that number, they picked you to go into the military. Like if you were one to one hundred, then it would likely be that you would go. But over one hundred, getting into the two hundreds, it was pretty much a given that you would not go to Vietnam.

My brother Jesse was nine years older than I was, so by that time, he was in his mid- to late-twenties, and he was already in the war. While growing up, there was a period that it was just him and me, and then nine years later, Chiquita was born and he was gone, so there was just the two of us. But by my Fisk years, he had been in 'Nam a long time. That was my second stroke of luck, I guess. They passed the policy that if there was a family member in the war zone, you certainly could get drafted into the army, but you wouldn't have to go over to 'Nam. I got lucky on both.

There were protests and heads getting beat in all around us all over again—now because of antiwar student demonstrations. We had won some victories as a race, but we found ourselves in a melting pot with the rest of America's problems to fix. Everybody learned in those Vietnam years that blacks, whites, Asians, and everybody in between all bled red the same. It was rumored that black men would deliberately be sent to the frontline. In fact, some years later, Stevie Wonder did a song by that very name that echoed the fears of a lot of brothers about Vietnam. How likely were you to not just be discriminated against in the military but tossed somewhere with less regard for your life's value? Don't think people didn't talk about it. Families of every color got a taste of death when their young ones didn't come back or came back half dead inside from war.

I certainly paid attention to it because my brother had been there a long time and still might have been there up until my final Fisk years. The war didn't officially end until 1975. Back in Gadsden, one of the biggest fears in the world during those years was a visit at night. A couple of times when we got a knock after dark, my mother almost passed out, knowing they would come at night and tell you that your child had gotten killed.

In my hometown, I think we had seven or eight young black men who got killed in Vietnam during the same period. It was certainly at the forefront of everybody's mind. When I was growing up, we had ROTC, which was for students who were military bound, and they normally were sent over with ranks like lieutenant, and that would often put them on the front of the lines where they would be killed. I knew a couple of college students who were ROTC who didn't return home alive.

Hundreds of colleges and universities across the nation shut down once all those students started those nationwide campus protests. Of course, we all felt something about Vietnam. Did I agree with that war? No. I thought it was a waste just like most of us did, but in that college era, I never did any formal protesting. All I had to do was remember what I went through in 1963, and I knew as I watched and supported them demonstrating that I would not participate. I focused on school and navigating my future in a time in America when everything looked ready to bust.

To give you an idea of just how active Klan hate was at that time, on November 26, 1973, my cousin was killed by a Klansman back in Gadsden. An enclave of Klansmen would gather at a bar across the main road—Broad Street—from where his house sat. One night while drinking, they agreed to find a black man to kill. The first house they came to with a black man happened to be right across the street, so they went over with guns. One Klansman knocked, and before my cousin could open it, the Klansman fired several times through the door, killing him. My cousin's three-year-old granddaughter was just a few feet away in the adjacent room and narrowly missed being killed. The Klansman was caught and convicted, to Gadsden's credit.

Such stories didn't filter to me while away at school at the time, yet in my eyes, they later proved me correct for why I left, especially because it was during an era when I was breaking white folks' rules left and right— particularly their dating taboos. I moved through my college years with this backdrop. I tried reaching for everything I felt I was missing when I was back home and wasn't eager to go back when it was over. When my parents came up on graduation day, I was slightly ashamed because I knew they were simple, working-class, down-home folks.

They were dressed in their very best and still were not shining next to all those fancy Fisk students' families, ones with money and prestige in my eyes. It's how I honestly felt, and that's the only way to approach this revisit to the past. The truth is, I had outgrown them. You must, to survive adulthood. There's a natural cord never cut, of course. But like the one on the telephone that rang in my parents' kitchen, my voice used it less and less to check in at some point. When Mom and Dad went home after graduation day, they took my long-term memories of "growing up Gadsden" with them.

PART IV

The Corporate Challenge

TESTING MY WINGS

I graduated and lived in Nashville for two years afterward. I stayed there because something happened to me my senior year. I tell my students at Texas Southern University this all the time—I was ill-prepared for the day after graduation, which is why I put so much emphasis on internships. Unfortunately, back then we didn't get the type of motivation or support from the university that they offer now—not enough to make us hone in. I was left with the question, "Okay, after you get this degree, what are you going to do?"

I have to say, my whole life follows that pattern of always having a job. Even in Chattanooga, I worked at a carpet mill running a forklift. Although very seldomly have I done physical work, I enjoy it, and I enjoyed living a good lifestyle from the money it made. I answered what to do next by going to an interview with a prominent air-filter company in Louisville, Kentucky. They had air-conditioning systems for hospitals in the surgical suite, which was important because of purification needs since infection is the number- one killer in surgery. Going to Louisville, they paid for the flight—my first as a matter of fact. I stayed at a hotel and the next day went through a series of highly intense tests that were required to get the job.

I would be the only black person in a class of thirty. I did well over the two-day testing program. Afterward, they said they would get back with me to let me know if I had gotten the sales position. On the second day, I went to lunch with three white guys, two of whom were administering the tests. The waitress came around and asked if we wanted something to drink, and they all ordered a martini. I said to myself, "Okay, if they're drinking that, I'm supposed to drink one too." I drank a martini for the first time not even knowing what it was other than seeing it on TV. They ordered another and then another. I joined right in. That's about as much as I remember of that lunch.

What I do remember is waking up in the hotel room and under the door was a note that said something like, "Based on what we're looking for, you do not meet our qualifications." They passed on hiring me after that. To this day, I'm convinced those Good Ole Boys were drinking water. I'm almost 100 percent sure it was a setup at least. How could it not have been? It's still happening today, that sort of setup for failure for black politicians, artists, and employees. It's no different now, and that is why staying vigilant and clearheaded is necessary while moving through that corporate playing field.

The next day, I took my second plane ride in life from Louisville back to Nashville, and I went to work at Meharry Medical College. They had a government-funded grant program that would take the doctors' kids who were eligible for the preschool program (three to six years old) and see what would happen when they mixed with low-income ones. I was the van driver who would pick up the low-income kids in the morning from where most of them lived—the projects and in poor neighborhoods. My position as a driver gave me a clear look at the lines between education and economics in ways I had never analyzed before. So even after leaving school, I was learning something that would be useful later.

The director of this program was an older woman who saw something and took to mentoring me. After this, I got an interview with IBM for a sales position—an interview unlike any I have ever had in my life. The district manager called me into his office. He closed his curtain, sat down in his chair, and had me sit in front of him on the other side of the desk. He started off saying, "Mathew, I want you to imagine that instead of age twenty-five you're forty-five years old. What kind of house do you live in at that time? Are you married? Do you have kids? How old are they? What kind of car do you drive? Do you have a pet?"

I answered all the questions. Afterward, he said, "I'm not going to give you an opportunity to think about this. You have to tell me right now. I don't have a sales position available, but I do have a marketing support position that I would like to offer you. You have to tell me right now if you accept."

I looked at him and said, "Sir, I'm a sales rep, and I want to be a sales rep and not a support person, so I pass on the position." After I walked out, I remember telling a woman what I said, and she screamed, "Are you *crazy*? You get an offer from IBM, and you pass on it?" Sure, I might have been feeling directionless before, but at least I knew what I wanted at that point.

HEADED TO HOUSTON

It was time for a fresh scene, and in October of 1976, I hooked up with some of my Tennessee State frat brothers and drove out to Houston. I saw the city for the first time, and I couldn't believe all the new opportunities that were opening there. Houston then had affirmative action, and in the 1970s, it was very oil industry dependent. If you could walk, talk, were black, and had a college degree, you had a job. It was a given because they had to meet their quotas in a quota-driven field. In the '70s, they did the massive hiring of mostly men and a few women as a result.

When I got there, I saw some of the guys I knew back in Nashville with lucrative jobs, driving nice cars, and living in amazing condos. I thought, *Wait a minute. This guy didn't even do as well as me in school, so how can he be living like this?"* Life became very clear to me at that point. I needed to move out to Houston. That's when the phone companies had the different names per region like Pacific Bell or Southern Bell and so forth. I couldn't transfer the job I had because there were two different Bell systems between where I was and Houston. I had to make that move with a leap of faith.

I worked it out with one of my fraternity brothers and his wife to let me stay with them in an extra bedroom. Because of frat brothers who they had previously let stay but ended up having to put out, I was under a thirty-day-maximum-stay contract I had to sign. I had the incentive to get it together quickly and get on my feet.

I always gravitated toward sales for a couple of reasons. I loved the fact that in sales you had the opportunity to have some flexibility in scheduling. I also knew in sales that people were making great incomes if they were good at it. I had a gift with the ability to persuade and communicate effectively with people, and sales offered that. I always knew that's where I wanted to be. When I got to Houston, I did a little research and narrowed my company choices down to two. I interviewed and trained with them simultaneously, getting paid training on both until I decided which one worked for me. I eventually decided and began my work at Pitney Bowles for about eight months.

A group of us sales guys who had come to Houston became quite successful, and we would get together on Fridays to mingle. It would be about a dozen of us at a bar in downtown Houston gathered to talk about the week. We often got very vocal about our strategies and successes, and one day we were overheard. A short white man had been listening to us black salesmen with great interest, and out of all of us in the group, he walked up to me.

"You know what? I've been listening to y'all. I'm impressed by you. How would you like to have a sales position at Xerox?" he asked me. He gave me his card saying he was over sales hiring. I ended up working for Xerox for the next ten years.

The transition was starting, and blacks were becoming more aware of corporate America. At that time in the country, something called Bid Rent Theory was taking place in major cities. The street repairs, policing, the fire departments—all of the better half of the infrastructure was being built outside of the inner cities. Therefore, you had this mad rush of white people to the suburbs because that's where there was an infrastructure. Plus, it satisfied those who wanted to be segregated from blacks. That was happening in America, and it led to the suburbs becoming populated by them.

Once we had elbow room with these new opportunities in corporate America, we had to come together to force change there. It wasn't going to happen by itself. That's why at Xerox, there were three major organizations for black employees spread throughout the South, the West, and the East. Our organization was called MUSR at Xerox—Minorities United in the Southern Region, and there was that similar type of organization out in California and the East. Xerox became a center focus once it was featured on the cover of a major magazine as the number-one corporation for blacks to work for in America.

Ours was the largest of the three organizations by far, and I brought in the 1980s as the president of MUSR for three years. We made effective and significant changes at Xerox for all black employees who worked there. It was rewarding to see black people moving into management and senior management, where before we had no equal opportunity for the better territories that existed, which were usually given to whites first. We also saw that more were hired for the company in those years.

Every quarter in my ten years at Xerox, I won a top salesman award. That started a leadership role and allowed me to begin training sales reps— working with at least twelve black sales reps from 1979 to 1980 alone. After a year of selling copiers, I applied to the medical division, where there were only two black salesmen. I don't think most of us even knew about it among the other elitist divisions Xerox had at the time. I went to the library for a month and studied everything I could on breast cancer because this product was xeroradiography, which was, at that time, a leading modality for that disease. I ended up interviewing and getting that position. That's when I noticed that there could be jealousy from my white counterparts in the business setting as well.

What they didn't know was that having entered in so many "first" positions throughout childhood on into my young adult life—integrating or hiring—that I developed a survival philosophy. When I'm the number-one sales rep, I can do whatever I want. When I'm number two, I know I might get fired because I'm black. If stayed number one, I did what I wanted in ways none of the others dared. When everybody else was wearing suits, I was wearing sneakers, blue jeans, and a T-shirt to the office

.

I also married in 1979 and started a family, and by 1980, I finally got that wonderful promotion into the medical division. Although I lived in Houston, I didn't cover it in sales. Instead, I found myself all throughout the southern part of Texas, which is San Antonio, Laredo, Brownsville, Harlingen, and McAllen. I also hit all the state of Louisiana as well as all of Tennessee and Alabama. Can you imagine what I was covering in those times not ten or fifteen years shy of those horrible lynchings and subsequent protests? These were major territories in the South, some of them notoriously racist, and it was a major culture shock. I had mouths to feed, so regardless, I did what I had to do.

I remember going down to McAllen, Texas, and not seeing any black folks—nothing but Hispanics and whites. It was probably a population then of about ninety percent Hispanic, ten percent white, and zero percent black. Any of the whites there worked in the oil industry, and they all had money. I would make some of my first sales calls there to the radiologists at their offices in the hospital or their personal ones.

When I visited one doctor, I came upon a Hispanic kid who, according to his reaction, had never seen a black person before. He was so excited he was jumping as he yelled, "Mama, el Negro, el Negro!" His mother was embarrassed, but I wasn't offended since I didn't know what that meant. I got used to that as I covered that whole Rio Grande Valley as we call it in Texas. I noticed that Hispanics treated me differently because they had rarely seen black people or had never had the chance to interface with any before.

In those days, I did fifty percent driving and fifty percent flying. In Tennessee, I drove through the mountains right outside of Chattanooga in Mount Eagle. I went to call on a radiologist there and made the mistake of driving my brand-new Jaguar to the city. As I walked out of my sales meeting, they paged me to go back and see the radiologist. He pulled me aside and told me, "Mr. Knowles, this Wednesday at noon, the Ku Klux Klan has their fundraiser downtown. So be careful!" We had these supersized cellphones back then, and I used mine to call my then-wife and told her, "If you don't hear from me in fifteen minutes, you call every police station you can think of."

It was that kind of narrow escape all over again— avoiding the very thing my family was hiding from in the bushes in Marion back in 1956. Each city offered up its version, so can you imagine what I was up against being a black sales rep in those states. Like in Louisiana, it is a different culture. The northern part of it, as opposed to the southern portion, is like two different countries. Once you get to Shreveport and Ruston, it's a sea of Baptist black folks with a closer-knit white/black relationship between them. You get to Lake Charles, Lafayette, New Iberia, Baton Rouge, Houma, and New Orleans, and it is as if you are in France somewhere.

Since I was covering the whole state, I had to go to poor, rural towns, where those impoverished people tended to be extremely racist. I'm talking about seeing pickup trucks with shotguns and dogs in the back and rebel flags in the windows. Remember, this was a different climate in the mid-1970s. Just coming out of major clashes with racists not a decade earlier, I was wise to be on my guard. I was very careful to have gas in my car in every major city so it would be full enough to get in and out of those little towns. Literally, it was to the hospital and out of there—period. I didn't ever want to be in one of them when the sun went down. Before I left the hospitals, I would have already used the restroom because I was not stopping either way. I would wait until I reached a major city to get a hotel room, and I made sure it wasn't one in the suburbs.

Just when I got more power in my position as the president of the MUSR organization and had plenty of fellow black employees that supported it, that's when a phenomenon started occurring. White women became part of the hiring quota. It began in the 1980s when we first got to hire black men, and then suddenly, some executives got around to actually reading the Civil Rights Act. When they did, they realized white women could be counted as a minority just like a black person could. Suddenly, you started seeing them honored in those top positions and in jobs that were formerly available to black men. Once the corporate system started utilizing that civil rights clause, you saw black men there less. However, after white women were hired, then black women followed, and that at least opened further opportunities in the community. On the other side of that picture is the devastating impact that it had on the black males in corporate America. After fighting so hard to get those civil rights laws in place for just such opportunities, what could you say if white women then counted as a minority too?

I never felt that my position was in jeopardy because I held the concept that the day I became number two, they could fire me. If I stayed the best at what I was doing, I figured nobody was going to fire me. I bargained on those corporate executives thinking, "I ain't got to like you if you make money for me." That meant we could all work together if everybody was making money. It was the same concept the coach at UTC had with us; it didn't matter if we were black if we helped them win. They didn't want us, but they didn't want to lose either. Since I was the president of the MUSR organization, in my mind I had a fiduciary duty to help my black counterparts fill not just sales positions but any advanced opportunities they had. I figured I had a duty to unselfishly look at how it impacted everyone and how I could be a leader and help them continue to better themselves. We'd all gotten that far, right? It was important to me to keep progressing. It was not all about just Mathew when I was in that organization, and I still feel passionate about my position.

(Xerox President's Club trip in Hawaii)

We had an alliance of black sales reps at Xerox that extended to any competitors' black reps, like at Kodak or IBM. It was like an unwritten but solid agreement between us that if I thought I was going to lose a potential customer, I would tell them, "You might want to call so and so over at IBM," and of course we'd naturally refer them to the black sales rep there. If someone were about to lose a customer at that company, he'd do the same. We had that kind of nonverbal pact that we were going to help each other even if we worked at different corporations.

Once I had achieved adulthood, a family, and a career making good money, I never stopped loving them, but I slowed down my visits with my family in Gadsden. I eventually asked my sister Chiquita to come, and she stayed for a year after I got her a good position at Xerox. I knew I wanted my sister out of the South and to taste that same freedom I got once I went to college. For my own reasons, I felt that city was a cesspool, and I didn't want her story to end up as one with no hope for her future. That was how I looked at her being there because I had gotten out for those same reasons. I love my sister and didn't want to see her going through all that I had left. Still, she wanted to go back home to Gadsden, even when I didn't understand why. Now, piecing her side of the story together, I can see a different perspective. The tallest building Gadsden had at that time was maybe six stories tall, whereas the ones in Houston might have been at least eighty. The competitiveness, the wealth of both black and white folks, the different city lifestyles, the speed...all huge contrasts that would have been intimidating. I understand now, but I still wanted what I thought was best for her.

By 1984 to 1985, when I was still at Xerox, I began to look at corporate America differently once my former wife and I started Headliners Hair Salon in Houston. It caught on and did very well and even expanded over time. Having an independently successful venture for seventeen years while keeping a foot in corporate America gave me the perspective I needed. By 1988 when they started closing a lot of those elite divisions at Xerox because they were losing money, I was headed for change.

The company president then became the president of another major medical diagnostic company. Just as they used to do with favored white executives, he did the same by taking me with him when he left. He took me with him because I was his number-one sales rep. Seldom was that done for black men at that time, and he not only took me with him, but he also paid me a lot of money. I don't know if I was the first black person in that field, but I never saw any others in 1988 selling CT/MRI scanners. Based on a recent conversation with a head operating nurse at a major hospital, there are still no black salesmen in those fields.

It was an overall positive experience for me at the corporate level, but because of my territory, it wasn't always a positive experience for my customers. When I did have to deal with racism, I used it to my benefit by making sure I would be so knowledgeable in that field that I could not be denied. We're talking in the medical field, which was different from selling Xerox copiers. When I would talk to a doctor, I had to know my stuff, and I was able to use my sales skills in that way. I also had the technical knowledge, which was beneficial, as well as having a firm financial background.

I walked into every sales call with the knowledge that I had to be better to survive. I had to be dressed and especially perform at my best. My mom had always said to me when I was at Litchfield Junior High, "You always gotta be better." I also had to be commanding. Just like she was tough and told that white insurance man to go back to his car until he could call her Mrs. Knowles, I learned to be assertive. I saw how some company associates wanted to be loud and funny in their customer pitches. But I knew I would gain trust by having a calming effect on my customers. I wanted that person to buy *me* first. And one of the ways they would do that would be to respect me, my knowledge, and ability. As a result, I was going to do fair business and assure them they could trust me if they had a problem later. I admit I did learn that from my parents and from those experiences I had growing up.

Along with the hair salon was another company we formed called Hair International Publications, Inc., and thereafter we specialized in oversized hairstyling books—in fact, three volumes of them at the time. I was still working in corporate America but also running this enterprise, which went on to make a million dollars a year with up to twenty-five hairstylists and assistants. Once it was a major company, I had investors coming to me. It could have been a turning point of its own had I stayed solely in that field, but I had other unfinished business.

From those college days when I made plans for starting groups and working in the music field, I was still very interested. It was an easy transition once I decided. That's when I started another venture—Music World Entertainment. Yet, in those first days of venturing out with just the two expanding businesses, I kept on doing medical sales. So, hold the image of those two self-owned businesses for a minute and fast forward a little bit to me acting as a sales rep for a major corporation. This experience was my last real foot in the corporate world during the days my other foot was itching to move on.

In this position, I only dealt with neurosurgeons by selling them the instruments they needed for surgery in the head and neck. This was highly sophisticated work. The hardest training I've ever done in my life was in this field, and I took classes right outside of Boston.

After one of the medical surgery procedures at Methodist Hospital in Houston, I was getting dressed when they paged me throughout the whole hospital. "Mathew Knowles, would you please go to Dr. Wilson's office?" I was scared. I thought I must have done something wrong in surgery like said something wrong or given the wrong advice on the equipment during the procedure. Something must have happened. As it turns out, the doctor wanted to explain something to me.

"You know, Mr. Knowles, I can't, unfortunately, use your instruments anymore because I got a directive from the administration here at the hospital that I had the highest-priced surgical procedure of any surgeon. And if I don't reduce my costs significantly, then I'm not going to have the opportunity to practice anymore." You see, that was the beginning of what we know of today as managed care; every procedure has a cost associated with it. I thanked him very much and said to myself, *You know, I don't want to do this anymore. I have no passion for this. Any blonde, blue-eyed white woman now can do this because it's not about quotas or their version of affirmative action. It's not even about quality. It's about cost. I don't want to sell cost; I want to sell quality.*

I had to decide. Was I going to do the hair magazine, or was I going to do the music management company I'd been dreaming of? It was between those two now because I was done with corporate America.

I made my decision and chose music.

MUSIC WORLD

Music was a persistent reminder of my future. In all those remote territories I covered, at least fifty percent of them for sometimes twelve hours was spent with me driving. What are you going to do? There was no cell phone; we had them then but the cost of using them was astronomical, so what would you do in a car? You only had one thing to do: listen to music. Those songs that reminded me of college also reminded me of the artists, the dreams I had, and even of my long-ago performances. Music was closer to me in my heart than I cared to admit.

I entered the music world, and although Beyoncé was a child and was singing by then, I wasn't yet focused on it at that time. Once her group went on *Star Search* and was beginning to get known, that certainly played a part in my decision. I didn't go at it lightly, having worked in business industries for so long. First, I did a DBA. I hadn't done a trademark yet, but I at least made an official move to get things started. I went back to Houston Community College, and I took artist management, music production, and public speaking courses just to help me begin to understand the business side of the industry. But I took it a step further by going to every seminar I could. I quickly realized something I had already known working in diagnostic imaging and sales: people buy people first. Second, it's about building those relationships and trust. That's what I started doing at those seminars—introducing and humbling myself to something new and wanting to learn.

Those were the first steps for me. I wanted to have a foundation of knowledge because I believe knowledge is power, and you don't just run out there with an idea and no clue. I took a room that we had in our house and emptied it out. It became my first office, and folks began to know me as I passed around my business cards with "Artist Management" on it. Eventually, a young artist, Lil O, sought me out, and I became his manager, getting him his first record at MCA Records. By the time I started managing what became Destiny's Child, I had fulfilled that pledge I'd made in college to one day start a girl group. I moved into life head-on and didn't look back at corporate America or my past.

ADVENTURES IN MUSIC WORLD

When I left the corporate world, I was a top salesman in my field. I had said early on that I would only do twenty years, and when I left corporate America, it was never to go back. No turning around. By now, I had a major hair salon in Houston and a unique hairstyling book—one of the first of its kind ever. It had caught on so fast and so hot it had me in entrepreneurship mode—as in the "I'm not into going back and working for someone else" mindset. That success made the decision between Hair International and the music world a tough one for me.

I knew then I had not come into the game to be on the sidelines; I came into the industry to be a player, and that was my constant mentality. I focused solely on the music business, and I was in no way intimidated by talking to record labels. I had been in sales, and a product/unit was all the same in terms of numbers. But instead of selling four-million-dollar MRI units, now I was selling the individuals and their talents. It was the same process—only now I had the people element.

It was one thing to watch my own back, but a young rapper and then a group of young ladies? Real lives still heavily benefited from my experience in selling medical equipment. Like when researching everything I could on breast cancer for days so I could be more informed when selling the equipment, I just had to remember there was a human element to all of it, and it helped avoid the real issues.

It was show business now. I had to be fearless. I didn't have any preconceived notions whatsoever about what it would be like. I went in seeing familiar lines drawn in that business too, and because I had stepped so fearlessly over earlier ones, I swiftly approached them when they stood in everyone's way. For the most part, every major record label had what they called a black or urban division then. There was segregation all over again when I first got into the music industry.

In those divisions, you rarely dealt with white folks; you dealt with the black or urban division—black department head, radio department, promotions, publicity, and marketing—and seldom did you interface with a white person.

What made me want to rip across the line was the difference in money as well as treatment. If I moved from a lucrative, half-million-dollar background in sales and my own hair magazine publishing business to do music, it would have to pay at least as much. And for a man who had held a job and worked to earn money since he was nine years old, I wasn't about to let racial lines stand between me and living well.

For example, where a new black artist's advance from a signed contract might be, let's say, one hundred thousand dollars, their counterpart white artist would get two hundred thousand. Their counterpart's recording budget might be half a million dollars compared to their one hundred fifty thousand. You had to have a video, and that might have been another one hundred fifty thousand dollars for black artists with three hundred thousand for the white talent. The marketing budget for a white artist would be at least one million while a black artist would get half that. It was a known fact that disparity and segregation still existed in the music industry. You wanted to make sure you connected with your base, and if you were a black artist, your base was usually black people. I realized back then you've got to first make sure you conquer your base, and then you get a chance with the mainstream once you do.

Since black artists didn't get a chance to deal with white people directly at the labels, it made it harder to cross over and get to pop music. Here is a breakdown of perspective and one I give my students at Texas Southern University where I teach entertainment recording management: Colorism again played a role, especially for black women who have done well at pop radio from Rihanna, Alicia Keys, Mariah Carey, Nicki Minaj, to others. Certainly, there are rare exceptions in any case, but let's examine recent landscapes in pop music to understand the color scheme so far. I do believe we have finally begun to grow out of those outmoded limitations based on colorism. This refreshed generation is changing a lot on many fronts, and we will see it soon in vivid color!

Yet I think this treatment of color and even deception against black artists is deep-rooted as well. It started with the music industry as far back Cadillac Records, which I learned a lot about when participating in the soundtrack for the movie. Based on the true story of Chess Records in Chicago, that movie really tells a story of white music executives from the North going down to the South and getting these guys on the cotton fields, who were great songwriters and great artists, and giving them a contract. That's why it's called Cadillac Records —they would give them a Cadillac and then take all their publishing, which is the number-one way you make income.

It was sharecropping in the way they could steal your royalties because they kept giving these advances. They would steal from the talent because many times some could not read well and/or the numbers would not be transparent, and so they took advantage of black artists. Favoritism based on racism and discrimination is still so prevalent that it runs over into the award nominations today. Don't take my word for it—listen to Adele's Grammy acceptance speech for Album of the Year. Even a majorly promoted white pop artist can point out the ongoing unfairness of how that category is awarded—decisions apparently still made behind a color line.

Once I found myself in my first big record deal, it was apparent to me that I was not going to like the separatist state of their divisions. I didn't understand it, so I thought just to bypass the black division head and deal with the president directly. I also understood how the game was played when it came to that whole belief that some of them had about my being both a parent and a manager. They had their minds made up at the door—"You're going to be emotional." Everybody is eager to point out Joe Jackson potential in every family-based manager. So the first thing I had to overcome was the idea that I would be limited because I'm a parent of a star.

It took a couple of incidents until they realized that I was smart enough to come up with winning strategies for my artists. By then though, I had the black people at the label concerned because I was dealing with the white executives directly. I was never intimidated about what I was doing because I had spent twenty years in a number-one position in sales, and I had learned to maneuver in the best interest of whatever was selling. Many times, I realized some of these guys never even graduated from high school, much less from college, but they were committed to success, so I had to carry this torch and be creative and strategic. *We should watch the Good Ole Boy network that's trying to hog all the money,* I thought. I'm not talking about the ones trying to do a good job; I mean the ones doing little or nothing to erase that line and who spent all day talking about sex, drugs, and other BS.

The business has changed drastically from what it was like in the 1990s, but back then, that's what it was like for many of us. I was trying to jockey for a position of respect because the money was blocked by the lack of it from those label heads who hid behind black executives at a desk. Ultimately, they phased out all those separated departments. I wanted one seamless avenue for the artists and the money they made. I would like to think that I had some impact in helping to change the concept of divisions based on race.

I would go off when I heard them say "urban" music. I would say, "Guys, stop the BS. To you, urban means black, and pop means white. So let's just be truthful about your thinking here; don't sugarcoat it." That just frankly pissed me off. I went in there against those unequal divisions from day one. I thought we should all be a team, and that team—white or black—should be a collective effort in using strategies for the artists to win—not just domestically in America but worldwide. That's why my artists have sold more records outside of America than here. I've extensively traveled outside the lines to sell my artists, and I saw once I went abroad that there were no urban divisions. That was how I thought it should be.

Using the strategy of breaking color barriers made the second Destiny's Child album so successful, and it crossed every barrier. This strategy resulted in a record without color limitations or those sharecropping options they had ready for many artists. It justified so much, seeing that crossover to pop charts worked so well and knowing that if they had boxed them into one demographic, things would not have been the same. It took away the barriers that existed between blacks and whites at radio stations too since that was the only way you could sell records. If you couldn't get radio, you would not be in demand.

Here is another comparison for perspective—one that I've always used on my first day of class at Texas Southern University for ten years. After my introduction, I address the class.

"I want to do a fundamental thing because we're going to use this the rest of the semester. Answer this: How many white people are there in America?" And I'm shocked and amazed how many young black students have no idea how many live in their own country. "Okay, let's call it two hundred million," I tell them. "Now, how many black people are there?" I'm once again amazed that they don't know. "Let's call it forty-six million," I say. "Okay, so how many Hispanic people in America?" Again, I'm shocked—they have no clue, so I give them the estimate of fifty-one million. For Asian people, I add twenty-one million, more or less.

I tell them this is critical and important. Most black people don't realize it's on average two hundred thirty million white people in America and only about forty million black people, give or take. From a businessperson's perspective, which size group do you want to sell to if you have a choice? Ideally, you want to sell to everybody. Trust me—my focus was on the 318 million combined. That was a deliberate strategy with my artists' pop chart crossover. From this point, I went and got a strategic relationship with Walmart, and teaming them with Destiny's Child was one of the keys to their marketing successes. I got to know the president of Walmart and the number-two guy there so well that I probably have been to Bentonville over a hundred times. I understood, even in 2002, that Walmart was the market king.

An interesting side note is that in the academic community, we like using what we call a white paper, and I published one via the University of West Virginia entitled "Strategic Partnerships with Walmart." Taking what I had learned in sales and the defiance for crossing limiting lines, I learned how to maneuver through that world with success. Yet, that much success so fast and so young…by the time you get to the top of whatever you have spent your life climbing, the view is startling. If you aren't ready, it can feel like you've only climbed as far as some dangerous edge.

FLYING WHILE BLACK

First-class life for me started with that second album of Destiny's Child in 1998. It was a busy and successful time, and I had moments of feeling comfortable, knowing some of the color barriers were moving out of the way. Is that how people in those formerly segregated communities felt in the years after the civil rights laws passed—tentatively taking the front seats of the bus, slowly getting used to enjoying the restrooms wherever they could find one, ordering a sandwich and not having to do it out of the back door or not at all? They, like me, might have eventually forgotten the separate signs and just relaxed into a sense of freedom. Can I let all my guards down? Maybe now, can we all get along?

At this stage, I was by any account more successful than ever before, having just closed a deal with a British company called Sanctuary, the largest independent record label and management company in the world, for several million dollars. I eventually became the president and formed a new division called Music World–Sanctuary Urban with seven hundred fifty employees worldwide and several million dollars backing it. I had 100 employees reporting to me from 2002 to 2007 between my offices in Houston as well as in Los Angeles, London, New York, and in Germany. That is when travel was even more expensive, yet every other day I was in either another city or another country for five straight years.

That set the stage for me to be a frequent and well-traveled flyer. I got comfortable in my new life but not in flying first-class thanks to what I came to expect as subtle racism. I traveled like many in the music industry—light and loose, not in suits, although we might occasionally wear one but not necessarily on an international flight. I'd be comfortable in blue jeans, sneakers, and a nice shirt. Back then, I also had an earring in one ear, so I really didn't look very corporate anymore.

Because of this combination and my race, I guess I was a magnet for the confused flight attendants. I can't even begin to tell you the times I've gotten on a plane, put my bag up, and looked up to see the flight attendant run over with, "Ahhh, sir! Sir, sir, sir, sir, that's reserved for first-class! You can't put your bag there!" I would look at them and ask, "So you just assume I'm not sitting here. Why?"

"Well, sir, I'm sorry the coach seats are back that way," they will usually direct me, and that's when I say, "Oh, by the way, I'm sitting in 3D." The reaction is usually embarrassment and occasionally an apology. That is flying first-class in the air. On the ground, anybody with a fancy car who happens to be black is undoubtedly profiled. Anyone who has experienced it will agree—it can happen anywhere, anytime.

Three years ago, I was leaving my office when it was just about dusk outside. I infrequently took my convertible Rolls Royce for a spin. It's more a treat than a daily occurrence to drive it, for which I'm grateful to have the opportunity, and this was one of those rare days. I was driving, top down, when I saw a cop rushing up behind me in my rearview mirror.

I pulled over as he stopped behind me and jumped out like he was having a coronary. He was sweating and nervous, almost choking on his breath, so naturally, I asked him, "Are you okay?"

All he could finally spit out was, "Is this your car?"
"Excuse me?"
"I said is this your car?" he asked again.

I told him, "I have two concerns. First, don't you mean, 'Is it your car, *sir*?'" (I get that from my mother, no doubt.) "Also, I didn't know it was policy to ask that. I thought the first thing you would want to see is my registration and my license. Why are you asking me if this is my car? Are you assuming I should not be driving it?"

He took my license and information and then stayed in the police car an incredibly long time. I'm sure he was trying to find out if I had any warrants or anything. It embarrassed me because by now, cars were passing by, and I was sitting in a convertible out in the open. It was almost forty-five minutes before this guy finished, and he came up and gave me a ticket for "crossing lanes at an intersection."

I said, "I've never heard of such a thing. Look, sir...all those cars are crossing lanes in that intersection. So why don't you just sit here and just give tickets out all day long?"

He shoved the ticket at me with, "Well, I'm giving you one for it now."

How could my parents and other black folks in the South have ever gotten comfortable on a bus seat still warm from the white man who wouldn't let them have it before? Nobody wants to be held back while trying to enjoy the quality of life they have earned. If I have the cash for first class, why wouldn't I be there if I wanted? But here's how dangerous they make that scenario: Michelle Obama said something profound when President Obama first went into office. The question she was asked was, "Mrs. Obama, are you frightened for your husband's life? Now he's the president of the United States. Are you frightened he might get assassinated?" She responded with something I'll never forget. She said, "No. I'm more frightened if he goes to the gas station and gets some gas." So what if I live in a luxury high-rise in downtown Houston or could drive such expensive cars—I am still aware that I'm a black man when I go to a white neighborhood. After a lifetime of reactions to my being there, it is engrained in my consciousness, and maybe that is the point they want to make —that it should be.

I'm blessed and grateful that I'm able to live in a nice building, yet when I get on the elevator with some of the wealthy white residents, I know how I'm perceived. I know at any given time, somebody, especially law enforcement, might get the wrong impression just like the officer that gave me that ticket. Now just imagine if I said something stupid or called him anything other than "sir."

A Rolls Royce has a perception of wealth that goes with it but not the image of a black man driving it (outside of chauffeuring somebody). That picture is all wrong. We don't sit for things like that in America anymore. This cop eventually was terminated because it turned out that he had profiled many others; I was far from the first. Some people would have just gotten their ticket, paid it, and went on. That's not me. I got in touch with the chief of the precinct and put my concern in writing, and he was considerate enough to follow up with me. I wanted action, and that's something that comes from the defiance still in me from my childhood. Some don't want to take the time or put themselves at risk for the action, but we should do that. You can't just accept the ticket and racism with it when they are clearly being written into the violation together. We can't live any longer with those kinds of actions. We must get them dismissed.

I learned a lot flying first-class, but while I seldom would see people who looked like me there, what I started noticing more were black pilots. It feels good to know they are flying those planes today and breaking barriers that, again in my youth, were unheard of. That makes me very proud. I have to believe some things, based on that, have gotten better for us because I think our economic power has gotten greater. I think we have people now in positions to empower the black communities like never before.

We deserve the same experiences our white counterparts are offered. It's as simple as that. I see improvement and growth when I travel now versus ten years ago. For us to grow, more education will be needed to bring about an ability for greater earning power. I see more black people getting educated thanks to the numerous ways we have today for getting a degree and continuing education. You can go online now and get education from a variety of informative platforms, including my Digital Masterclass, "The Music Industry in the Digital Age." I see that type of growth happening in America, and I'm hopeful.

I wonder what people like the flight attendants or that police officer who doubted my status saw when they looked at me, a black man. Did they see someone who had emerged from farm workers and who had himself picked both tomatoes and cotton as a child? Did they see someone who had emerged from the South as a victim or a survivor? And for that matter, did my own growing family see the residual effects of what I had experienced as a youth? Did they see a high achiever who made it in spite of it all?

I adopted a winning philosophy in my life as law, developed no doubt first by my mother from those days when she raised me to always push for the best. Why would they need a second-rate minority token around? It would be easier to just fire me and keep up the Good Ole Boy network for as long as possible. I simply had to get all those number ones wherever I could find them and the rewards that came with them. That was the prize for climbing out from under their hateful thumb. That was the treasure found by digging past the tricks and limitations.

That reward includes the images I gained later on magazine covers. Those pictures of a beautiful family and empire were shining examples of everything number one could earn—in spite of the limitations. Who or what could take that right away? Well, I'll tell you. If nobody mean-tempered is around to fight you for that new life...if the trauma, negative treatment, and fear have only been covered up and never healed, you might do it to yourself and not even know it. You will lose it if discrimination is a seed that grows in you, bringing on pain right when the shine is brightest and all eyes are on you.

All those rewards start to look like either stones or seeds that fall at your feet. The stones hurt, but you can keep on marching across those. If the seeds are negative, they'll sprout right when you comfortably adjust yourself at the front of the bus and take a nap. Those seeds from my childhood had potential weeds choking out some part of the successful me. They sprouted up right on my perfect, million-dollar lawn. I got overwhelmed inside and needed clarity. The climb to get ahead, the work to maintain it all, the fight to preserve respect from everyone around me became weeds everywhere. If you come into the soul-devouring arena of show business carrying any baggage with untreated traumas in it, expect to need some support, if not therapy, before long.

Drugs, sex, and rock 'n' roll are as old as the business itself, and they keep us weeping in the headlines over fallen stars. My experience, while hard, has a better ending than a lot of those who didn't survive their toxic cocktails of art, fame, and money. I paid then and still do for that shiny life under headlines full of tabloid untruths and cockeyed speculations. I learned the hard way that if they want a bad guy, they will build a bonfire out of your mistakes to roast you. That's the optic the public receives in exchange for that first-class ticket you buy. What's the cost for all that? For me, it was about twenty years of on-and-off therapy and a lot of inner reflection on family and my past. Going into therapy, I had hopes of locating some forgotten part of myself. A puzzle missing a piece isn't broken—it's just incomplete as a picture. In therapy, I fished out these frames of my forgotten past and looked closely.

It showed me the defiant jump into the falls had never stopped for me. I would risk it all to have what I wanted, and I had gotten it so many times just that way. The fall was my inner rage—and there was a lot—that let me leap so easily into danger and in defiance of their limitations time and time again.

HOME IS WHERE THE HURT IS

Now I understand something...

I understand the reason my daughters did not need me to be a part of their careers anymore. It was for the same reason that I didn't want to be around my parents after I left home. My daughters needed to go out on their own and make it happen. I had given them what they needed, just as my parents had inspired me way more than they knew before I broke free. I didn't go to Gadsden for Christmas or any holidays after I left—none of that—and my parents didn't visit me either. I thought of graduation day and how I was so scared they were going to embarrass me, how I made sure we did our thing quickly and left. I just voluntarily sent them money, though they didn't ask, and did my best to get my sister to leave there.

That need to escape Gadsden was really at the root of my desire to leave something buried in my childhood there. It surfaced all at once, and it is what led to the therapy. The symptoms of the inner stress began years before I entered the hectic pace of show business. It was the early 1980s, and a lot of things happened. Reverend Walker, my childhood mentor, died. I also got married, and we moved into a new house, all while I was being promoted to a new position. As exciting as that all sounds, those are the most stressful things that can happen in one's life. Those are well known as the most traumatic events that can occur psychologically, and all of that happened to me within a six-month period or less.

When I first got my promotion, I began having these incredible anxiety attacks. I had to go to a medical doctor because my palms started sweating hard, and I had a shortness of breath. When I began that job, I would have to go into radiology departments or hospitals, and in the 1980s, they were usually in a basement. The color was puke green, and the lights were always dim and shadowy. Their radiology staff would park patients in a hallway until it was time to go to X-ray. They would then lie there, and I would be left alone with them until they called me in to do my sales pitch. It psychologically bothered me to hear these people moaning there by themselves—that and the sick, green lighting effect of the painted cement walls.

Also, it was the first time that I started flying that frequently; at that point, I was flying two times a day. I was in three to four different cities per week because I had such a large territory, all with this fear of flying as well. I had to wear a twenty-four-hour EKG device because the doctor wanted to know what was causing the anxiety attacks, and this would help me log them. He could see the log and determine if I was having a heart attack or something else and at least how it was physically affecting me.

Once I had spent a month doing this with a regular doctor, he said, "Mr. Knowles, this is something psychological; it's nothing physical that's happening with you." That is when it was recommended that I go to a therapist. It was the 1980s, and the news headlines were no less stressful than the ones from the '60s or '70s with more of the same. Nobody was completely immune to the struggle and stress. It wasn't common in our community to seek therapy or treatment for anything other than physical symptoms, yet the other option was my default when I didn't. A successful life can offer you any number of things with which to cope, and I used alcohol and even sex and excessive work to cope with mine. Those were the things that could get me off the trauma train inside. What was internally bothering me that I hadn't dealt with?

During that initial treatment back in the early '80s, I got a diagnosis of impulsive behavior with the effect that anything I do, I do to the extreme. If I'm playing basketball for fun, I'm going to play basketball to absolutely win. Work, the same thing. Planning, same thing—all or nothing. That was diagnosed before I had an even busier and more demanding schedule than I ever had in sales—when I entered an industry that pushes everyone to be number one. I had many experiences in the music world before I had time to dig any deeper into anything I might have buried in my past.

(Gordon Parks, photographer. Dr. Kenneth Clark conducting the "Doll Test" with a young male child, 1947.)

EROTICIZED RAGE

A true diagnosis didn't really happen for me in therapy until the late 1990s. At this point, I had already been in therapy since 1981—so about a decade and at least a million dollars over those years. It took that much time and money just to locate someone who could truly help me sort through all these fragmented pieces of my life and form a picture I could live with for the rest of it—without the internalized traumas. Before I had my breakthrough, the therapy sessions were sugarcoated and surface from my end and the therapists'. None of us put a shovel to the BS and dug deep.

I started out with one who was a first timer at it, and so was I, and I think neither one of us knew what we were doing or how to go about it. It wasn't continuous over those ten years; only when things got out of control, would I go back to therapy. I eventually met a Jewish female therapist that I ended up staying with for quite a few years although still not continuous. I've always looked at therapy as a tool, and when I needed it, I would get it. The tool would give me clarity, balance, and direction. It became a roadmap for what I needed to do.

I don't think you can get that from a friend. I think it requires someone who is trained just for the same reason. I have a tremendously supportive and wonderful circle of friends and mentors I consider close, but I wouldn't go to a buddy if I had a stomachache or needed surgery. He is my friend, but that's not what he does. I want to go to somebody who specializes in what I need, especially when what I need is that internal shovel. If I have some emotional or psychological issues, I need specialists, not buddies.

I was seeing this therapist when the racial dynamic surfaced again, and that shifted me into the direction that led to my ultimate progress. As a part of my therapy, a series of men's groups of all ages, sizes, and colors were available to join. In my groups, there were always men my age who were affluent. Any number of highly ranked executives for major companies or those who owned their own businesses would be there. That was our commonality—success. We faced similar challenges that way, and while our traumas might have been different, the results in most cases were the same. Like for some of us, our behavior had begun to overflow into our marriages—certainly, that happened to me.

The therapist made a prophetic statement a couple of times when she mentioned both the downside and the upside of my reaction to the traumas. "The bad side," she said, "is that you overdo things. You sometimes drink too much, you sometimes party too much, your taste for women is too much. But the good thing that came out of this is that you would have never been as successful were you not." She truly believed that, and I do too because I would never have been as driven. There is a personal, professional, and spiritual part of me, and I think my past struggles enhanced my professional performance in that way. On the flip side, my choices and my excesses then became clearer as I recalled how my mother had always conditioned me as a child. *"Don't ever bring no nappy-headed girl up in my house."*

Do you know that command, plus the obvious fact that I couldn't have a white girlfriend according to her and the law of the land, both, made me want one more? It became something that had a clinical name to it—eroticized rage. Such an unconscious conditioning affects any number of men who go after race as the primary basis for their romantic choices. For them, in frustration of what they are socially denied, it is an act of vengeance to get what is considered taboo. I can look at my teenage years and those stolen moments atop Lookout Mountain as prime examples. It reminded me of an earlier experience.

It was still a risky time in the South, and I continued finding a line to step over, even if I wasn't aware of it. When I moved from Nashville to Houston, on my drive there, I had a secret encounter with a young lady whose father was the dean of a major college in Mississippi. I spent the holiday with her in secret—in his house on campus. I was basically under his nose and taking the worst risk ever. Had I have been caught in this particular white man's house, the outcome might have been a lot worse than only seeing his angry, red face. I was done with risks of that nature in a part of the South that wasn't progressing as fast as the rest of the country on civil rights or economics. I was ready for a change.

I think back to when I met my first wife. I thought she was white, although she never claimed to be. I'm just talking appearances and first impressions. I quickly saw her beauty and blackness inside and out. According to my sister, even after my mother met my future in-laws, she stayed convinced all of them were white. I'm sure she didn't mean for me to bring one home but considering my choice in women's complexions based on the colorism she passed on, I almost did. There was this idea in America that if you had even a small percentage of African blood, you were black. One drop. It didn't matter if you were mixed so far down you could pass if you wanted to. There was still that fact, and even those fairer-skinned black people had racism shoved at them.

I got to see it once while driving from Houston through Chattanooga with my then-wife when we stopped to get gas and she asked a white man for the restroom. He snapped at her rudely, "We don't have one!" That response showed me we were all in the same pot, even if it was melting with a variety of shades.

I now look at my beautiful wife Gena with pride for her intelligence and grace as well as admiration for her lovely brown skin. I realize I first began liberating from my mother's coloristic conditioning during those therapy sessions. What has come out since, in my research, is how systemized such thinking was in our culture—and still is in some places. The harshest form of racism was making us hate ourselves and internalizing the slave owner's dislike of our looks and skin tones. This was planted along with any number of other seeds that grew up in our community through generations. *Hate your own kind for me when I'm not around*—that's what that taught us. My mother was a victim like many others who got the same conditioning. Yet, it was meant to disregard the one thing you're born with—the one thing hardest to get rid of—your race.

Besides those two breakthroughs, I was still not shoveling deep enough under the traumas; I was just hovering near. The therapist did help me shovel at the ugliest parts, and we had accomplishments with that. Back in those men's group sessions, I noticed there were a lot of young men in the group, and for some odd reason, I was always the only black guy. In one session, a young man in his mid-thirties whose father owned a prominent grocery store chain joined us. There, we were asked to look at one another in the group and say whatever role we thought everyone represented. You were to say whatever came to mind first. This guy looked at me when it was his turn and repeatedly said, "You're a nigger." I was calm, but you could tell everybody was disturbed by it.

That's when I sought out a black therapist, whom I kept using the rest of the time I would need therapy as a tool. I kept telling my white therapist that she couldn't identify with this area. I explained that I needed somebody black who could help me relate to this racism issue I had buried. What she had spent ten years trying to do I was able to speed through with the help of a therapist who is also an ordained minister. He has been involved in counseling for more than twenty-five years. This helped me enter group therapy with men who not only matched my career status and age, but also, out of ten men, seven or eight were black.

It was like night and day because we could talk about things we could all relate to, and often that topic was racism and how it affected us. I guarantee, in every group therapy, race came up. It was a diverse gathering with bright minds, like with one being an educator and another an executive, all coming from various walks of life. It transformed the men, all of us, because even with the white men participating in group, we eventually saw personal breakthroughs as well. Some would say, "I never looked at it that way." One guy told us, "You know I'm not a racist. I thought about what you guys said last night. And then I realized that when I saw my friend John, the first thing that came to my mind is, *He's black.* I never thought about that before. I thought I looked at everybody the same, but I thought, *He's a black guy who is my friend,* not just, *That's my friend.*" We helped others who had never seen that those lines needed to be erased also.

THE AFTER-EFFECTS OF TRAUMA

Once you hit a wall, you bounce back to whatever made you run so fast you didn't see it coming in the first place. For many people, it's their past or something buried down in it. I knew the racial traumas of childhood and the sometimes subtle, often loud, bigotry I faced in the corporate world all had an effect. Once I had entered a phase of success and affluence, it would seem I had overcome my limits in remarkable ways.

Even without encountering any racism daily, I had internalized much of that trauma. What success at a certain level will do is expose it. You see, I had left my hometown, but pieces of it had never left me. They were the ugly patches at which nobody ever wants to look—the ones that make you ask "Why?" as a child. I can only ask these questions here down the line. Back then, I didn't bother because I was too busy growing up in an era that taught us anything could happen to a poor black kid in America. Period.

I remember traumatic events like going to a dentist for the first time and waiting anxiously in the colored waiting area. Eventually, the white dental assistant took me to the room with a dental chair. My mother was not allowed to accompany me to the room. Without a word to welcome or calm me (I was obviously scared), I was left alone for what seemed like hours. I sat alone staring at the needles and instruments, listening to the unfamiliar sounds with the type of fear that only a young child alone can have. It was in no way a comforting or welcoming experience for a child in a segregated setting with medical staff lacking in even basic bedside manner.

The effects of that day and those moments have led me, in some of my therapy sessions, to review long-term trauma based on seemingly innocent events. Even today, I have a tremendous fear of dentists. Trauma works in such a way that it can linger for years. I fully understand how someone assaulted over thirty years ago can revisit and finally want to address it. In many ways, I can relate to that.

With the traumatic events happening around us today, it is extremely important that each of us show social courage. Social courage is when we take a stand against racism, sexism, xenophobia, and homophobia. It can be in our workplace, marketplace, home, or school where we say "No" to any negative beliefs and views being expressed.

PART V
OUTRO:

RACISM
TODAY

ROOTS & BRANCHES OF HATE

[1]rac•ism
noun
Prejudice, discrimination, or antagonism directed against someone of a different race based on the belief that one's own race is superior.

prej•u•dice
noun
Preconceived opinion that is not based on reason or actual experience.

xen•o•pho•bi•a
noun
Intense or irrational dislike or fear of people from other countries.

sex•ism
 noun
Prejudice, stereotyping, or discrimination, typically against women, on the basis of sex.

ho•mo•pho•bi•a
noun
Dislike of or prejudice against homosexual people.

1Britton, Ronald. 2017. "Internal Racism: A Psychoanalytic Approach to Race and Difference." *International Journal of Psychoanalysis* 98, no. 2 (April): 543. Blackwell Publishing Ltd.

A simple, honest look in the mirror will help you see if any of those definitions fall into your belief systems, attitudes, or actions. If so, these are the times that will challenge you to acknowledge them. Or just simply let an innocent child's eyes be your mirror.

After my experience with them, I might have thought of the Klan as the bastions of racism, but I found they are not alone by far. Once I saw them with my own eyes as a child, I grew up trying to spot them outside of their white sheets and as a result learned that racism could be subtler and any-damn-where. How many people harbor the trait that does not fit the typical image of a bigot? Through each subsequent year of my life, particularly throughout the 1960s and mid-1970s, I would see just how many ways it could exist. It persisted from colorism found within my college community—as in light versus dark—to self-directed and internalized racism I picked up in the corporate world. In this new era, a hot topic has also come up with increasing numbers of white people also claiming they face instances of "reverse racism."

With landmark decisions on the topic made by the Supreme Court recently, whether in the court-upheld University of Texas affirmative action decision to admit minorities over similarly or more qualified white applicants, or even with the lawsuits rejecting those complaints, these cases may prod us into addressing such talk more openly.

As well, 2Asian-Americans suing Harvard over their admission limitations for their group show us that all over, race relations are taking on broader dimensions. When the US Supreme Court agreed that workplace discrimination had indeed taken place with white firefighters, their lawsuit win opened the door to a reexamination of modern racism in the workplace like never before. In that case, when no black firefighters qualified for a promotion, the city declined to issue any promotions at all, causing the white group to sue based on reverse discrimination.

---

[2]New York Times. 2017. "Affirmative Action Battle Has a New Focus: Asian-Americans." http://www.nytimes.com/ 2017/08/02/us/affirmative-action-battle-has-a-new-focus-asian-americans.html?searchResultPosition=2.

Many argue that whites aren't often found to be victims of any form of racism until you start to examine more closely the discriminatory and judgmental treatment of Jews, Albanians, Romanians, Serbians, and the list goes on to sometimes include genocidal actions taken against them based on racial castes and sub-ethnic clashing—all within the spectrum of same-race relations.

As I moved through corporate America, I could see such racism among members of the same groups and noticed how those prejudices affected them as well. Often, what I got once I moved from the South and into higher regions of the corporate world and even began traveling the globe was the subtler form of racism. Nobody dropped telltale flags along the road beneath my feet or honked a horn to announce their hate. You just felt it. Whether it is the doubt about my assigned seat in first-class when I'm flying or waiters and store clerks who assume what I can or cannot afford—it's out there.

Even Oprah, one of the richest women in the world, has experienced overt "You don't belong here" treatment when shopping abroad. The media stereotypes don't help, and those are what we fought diligently to dispel during those early civil rights years when educating white America about who we were and what we could do was so necessary. In my years renting and then buying property, I could see the quiet racism in the eyes of landlords. As an employee, it was in the hard gaze of a few co-workers and hiring executives. It is an undercurrent of meanness that may hide behind a smile that stops at the eyes (polite to a point), and I spent decades trying to decipher it.

Even now, perhaps the hardest to witness are racist attitudes that run black on black. From the movies *Imitation of Life* to *The Color Purple*, and Spike Lee's *School Daze*, the underbelly of how some learned to view their skin tone, hair texture, features, etc., has always been with us. This pushes many toward augmenting or adjusting them to the point of nonrecognition. Because these ideologies are still prevalent, skin bleaching is now an epidemic in countries like India, the Caribbean, and Africa, and the fads among the rich feed the acceptance. It is something to grow up in an era that held up fists and declared, "The blacker the berry, the sweeter the juice," to now see the new trends set on draining that blackness out. I'm not judging them as much as pointing out this evolution so we can ask, "Where is this going, and better yet, where did it come from?"

I came up through an era with blonde and blue as the Hollywood standard into another era watching afros rise as high as the black fists, and now I see the metamorphosis of a new generation, mixing it however the hell they want to. I raise the speculation that if the new bleaching, nose surgery trends are based on that same spirit of colorism we knew from slavery days, then it has never stopped. It means internalized racism has been projected, blasted, preached, and instructed to so many generations that it's apparent it won't easily go away.

For example, if a person intentionally marries someone of another race— not out of love, but to ensure their offspring are as ethnically different in appearance as possible—is that colorism bred from internalized racism? If a man has the mindset he is inferior, lacking in all ways next to his racially different counterpart and therefore performing poorly all through life, is he a victim of self-directed racism? There were once cotillions based on color—the Blue Vein Society (where you had to see the vein clearly under the skin to get in), the brown paper bag tests, and so on. Even when my daughters were children, someone approached us and asked us to enter them in a similar setup. We declined, mainly because what signal are we sending to the children, and what ideas are we perpetuating among adults who practice it?

The children left out of such reviews are still moving through our families, schools, and societies under the yoke of not only subtle differences, but also overt prejudices about their color. Colorism can be found based on darker skin whether in the Hispanic, Asian, Indian, or African American communities. But where did it come from? Where will it go? Isn't it time we asked? Going back to that racist root, we see the colorism branch stemming directly from notions of white supremacy. The Rwandan genocide between the Hutu and the Tutsi people show how color differences were manipulated, leading to ethnic disparity and genocidal war. It wouldn't be the first time in history, and sadly it won't be the last. Racial profiling says, *"That guy looks like he's gonna do something bad; go stop him before he does"* while stereotypes help feed the idea.

There doesn't have to be a cross burning in your yard for you to experience racism. Snubs, slights, denial of basic rights or services, ridicule, and harassment based on your skin color place those acts under subtle racism. In each phase of my life, I faced and maneuvered around these various forms of hate. I realized meanness didn't just pick a color; it could morph into any other version of discrimination and hatred. Once one form of hate takes root, the branching moves to subgroups, such as women, gay people, or foreign-born folks. Once I understood meanness didn't just wear a white sheet or a label so clearly defined as "racist" and it could be found in many other forms of prejudice, I grasped that what I had seen through innocent eyes as a child was only the beginning.

In 2017, I went back to Gadsden. I met with relatives and cruised old blocks taking photos and piecing together the final outlook. Meanwhile, in the news, racism is a major headline all over again. Within the months following the presidential election of 2016 and then the New Year and on to what is now the writing of this book in winter 2017, several incidents have taken place with echoes from the past. I'll focus on just these last months as an example. Twice in the same week, a noose was found on the Smithsonian grounds at the National Museum of African American History and Culture. Two more were since placed there.

I could bullet point numerous such dangerous incidents from 2017 headlines, yet a few truly stood out for me during the writing of this book, such as a deadly stabbing by a white supremacist over racial slurs involving a young woman wearing a hijab, the riots and tragic replay of segregationist times by openly hostile white supremacists in Charlottesville, the immigrant hostility, and the very tenor of the Alabama Senate elections between Roy Moore and Doug Jones and how it galvanized black women of the state in particular to turn the final, seemingly impossible vote. My mother would have been there among them, voting for what's right, and my parents would be proud of what the black folks of their state showed the entire country. I flew to Gadsden to participate in raising a voice in that election, and it was heavily tinged with elements from the past.

This progress even as the ever-controversial battles on social media between citizens who oppose racial bigotry and those who practice it vocally rage on. It isn't just discrimination against one's race that is heating up the headlines either; sexual harassment and gender prejudice as well as deep-seated homophobia is much discussed. It, too, is as old as racism.

I recently met a white fellow from Gadsden who is my same age and has now relocated to Houston like me, and he told me his reasons for leaving and never going back—homophobic persecution. As an openly gay man, he felt no desire to ever go back to that energy of the South, and he told his own tales of discrimination. I realize the fight has gotten broader. The Dakota Pipeline has prompted the Native American community to take another visible stand, and it is back in the news after what looked like a victory. In their way, they're still fighting Andrew Jackson's mean.

I picked up these various headlines while flying from city to city where I have more "flying while black" experiences over the five flights in three days I traveled. It was enough after a while until I was honestly sick of it. At one point, after hours of delay already, I stood in an airport trying to get a flight attendant to own up to her discriminatory treatment. I challenged her on whether she would have held up the flight for a group of tourists from Nigeria the way she did for a group from Portland, making everyone wait for this group's accommodation.

This was after having observed her total disregard for the rest of us with a flight to catch. I realize these subtle racists don't even see us. We must speak up. It set into motion one final burst of defiance because I realized something—how necessary it is for us to not be complacent. I see so many just accepting this treatment around me when if nothing else, those occasions are teachable moments. So, you just did something foul, and it smells like racism. Am I supposed to just let you pass and go contaminate the rest of society? It's like what I witnessed growing up—seeing the ones who seemed afraid to speak up or act out to come protest with us or picket some place that discriminated against them too. Fear of losing a job, fear of police reaction and the resulting pain, fear of the offending racists themselves, fear of death—whatever the reason, I see it still there.

So much of what we talk about in private together is how often this treatment happens to us. That's how slaves had to behave, sitting in secret talking about the evil of Ole Massa in fear of their lives, unable to say anything to his face. Now that we can speak up, it's still mostly done in private where it's a hot topic among us these days. The mistreatments, slights, disqualifications, subtle denials, passed-over opportunities, name calling, disenfranchisement...it goes on and on, and yet the ones who need to hear about it the most are the perpetrators. As soon as I see it, it's never about complacency —not for somebody raised in an era where that sort of tolerance kept us down, not raised by a mother who would send a white man back to his car until he could come back carrying some respect for his policy.

"We treat everybody the same," is the line they all give me, no matter what airline, no matter what city. "You wouldn't tell Kris Jenner that," I shoot back. A white celebrity paying first-class money is usually the first person they comfortably accommodate over everybody else—even just as the parent of a celebrity. Until it's a black man, then he's all too often mistaken for that "anybody." After he's climbed his way through so much to get to that well-paid seat, it's an insult. After an already three-hour delay and after days of travel, it's an outrage. Occasions like these—and more frequently on airlines lately—are signs of how such tensions in tight spaces are bound to collide. As of this writing, there was a very public headline I caught on BBC News online where they quoted the NAACP warning African Americans against just such discrimination with one specific airline. I could completely relate.

It has bubbled to the surface in many of us just like that —young and old, black and white, rich and poor. With some speaking out, marching, protesting, holding up signs and fists, singing protest anthems made for a new generation—that's what "Woke" is all about—it's the end of that closed-lip complacency and the end of timidity that won't make offenders walk back out and start all over again with some respect. We've earned that by now.

You will see this mix of anger alongside even more complacency and finger-pointing with more feet taking it to the street before racism delivers any final bows, as if it ever could. An excellent outlook on that is found in author Derrick Bell's *Faces at the Bottom of the Well*. It is a telling dialogue about racism's permanent, dyed-in-the-wool effects on us all and our role in dealing with that today. This mindset has deep roots and quickly sprouting branches that move in every direction—into institutions, splitting through homes, up through politics, tearing across religions, and pushing into the people themselves to make them internalize their traumas. That's a lot of work for all of us. But I come from parents and grandparents who faced back-breaking work head on every day of their lives because that's what you do to keep you and your family alive. I bet many of you readers do to. We know in our blood that there is no place for complacency in that mindset or else you starve.

Racism has branches running into the wealthiest and most-watched arenas in America right now. You can bet the children see it. How many are being told to "Go back to__" ? That blank can be filled in with Africa, Mexico, or Pakistan these days. How many are watching the N-word battle playing out like a basketball game with it being passed back and forth along the court of public opinion? It's in the songs blasting on the speakers everywhere because it's mainstream music on one side, and then it spills out of Bill Maher's lips, and it's headline news on another. You don't have to be a child to be confused when even the president calls Haiti and Africa a shithole.

And then within that same ten-day span, one of America's biggest star athletes, LeBron James, had the N-word splattered across his luxury home by racists. In response, he said something that drove home whatever success I thought I had gained by being away from Gadsden and in the spotlight, flying commercial or first-class, in a Rolls Royce or an Uber. As Lebron said, "No matter how much money you have, no matter how famous you are, no matter how many people admire you, you know being black in America is tough. And we got a long way to go, for us as a society and for us as African Americans, until we feel equal in America."

Yes, there is hope. This generation is defying so many of the limitations previous generations set. The same night I had that aggravating experience in the airport, just as I was exiting, there was a small boy who stopped and held the door for me. I was so startled to see a white kid giving this older black man what so many adults had just ignored—common courtesy and kindness. I was so moved, I went and sought out his parents and told them so. "Did you know your son did this for me?" I asked. It was two a.m., the wee hours after a long and frustrating day of flying while black. I was glad to tell them how his simple act of kindness had lifted my spirit, and whether I told them or not, it gave me a profound understanding—that yes, there is hope for us all.

As I drove through Gadsden, I recapped my picturesque journey through childhood, revisiting each of those landmarks from the past. This place was a piece of America. Beauty was struggling to grow up against the ugly with the help of great men like my cousin Robert Avery. One last drive through Gadsden gathering that closure reminded me of the purpose of my defiance. I drove fearlessly down streets where, for me, the lighting was still all wrong. There were too many shadows, and the color was just off. The courthouse, the church, the railroad tracks...all were landmarks of the past now. I left Noccalula Falls where I could lay some of that defiance inside me to rest before a ride up to Lookout Mountain. I stood there looking at that view, not as a brave or a warrior, but as a man who was once a boy not even aware he was trying to make a stand. That unknowingly defiant risk to find some love was courageous anyway.

I drove past the old produce store and saw the yard where the delivery truck would pull up when Big Mac got done working. His big smile was always in place for everyone he passed. Our old house was gone, and the lot was empty of his collection of old buses full of found things. I made sure I visited our old plot and saw where our house he built once sat. The other, which he rented out and was ultimately sold to the same family, still stood. The owner was full of stories about things he would do, and she remembered him with a smile. He had that effect on people, and she was a nice reminder. What a big man—at heart and in life with all he did.

I imagined him on that porch where folks could hear him singing to his grandkids: "*Daddy's gonna buy you a mockingbird....*" I thought of my daughters and the extended time they spent there with him and my mother when they were small enough to fit on a knee. What he gave them, instead of a mockingbird or a looking glass, was a song from his heart, and I hope they still can hear it over life's noise. If so, keep it in a bank and never spend it no matter what. I could smell my mother's cooking into which she said she put her love, and I heard the music that made us dance. In other words, I collected the beautiful parts before I left too.

I drove to brighter areas on the way to meet my cousin and his wife, who at age fifteen spent three days as a youth protestor in the jail that summer of 1963. The two married and raised a family while contributing to sweeping changes throughout the government and the schools in Gadsden. One building at Carver High School even carries the family name —the Bettye J. Knowles Gallery. That tradition continues in Houston with the Knowles-Temenos Place Apartments.

I broke bread with Robert, who still courageously works to make massive and ongoing changes to a system that never beat him enough to stop him or drive him away from the task. We all shared many reflections that helped me bring together elements for this book. After I spent the end of the trip with family at dinner, full of the meal and the memories, I got ready to close the book—for these chapters at least. I know a fuller autobiographical scope will no doubt follow with all the rest of the story, details still untold.

Then I was ready to leave. After goodbyes that didn't feel as distant as they once did, I got in my rental car and headed to Birmingham. That's where I planned to grab a hotel before I flew back to the life I carved out, having escaped any attempt by my past to carve the life out of me.

I still won't sleep in Gadsden—not yet, not even if they built a five-star hotel with my name on it. Maybe that's just the child in me, still seeing the shiny-helmeted troopers coming over the hill with hot fire in their hands in the form of a prodder.

I have thought about, and still may as of the writing of this last chapter, meeting with my cousin Oscar Underwood in Marion, Alabama, to retrace even older steps than our parents, perhaps to challenge him on that return to a place where he too can sew together pieces of that quilt he first pointed out. We can both appreciate all the academic roots in Marion and the entrepreneurial spirit we inherited from it and maybe see the changes from the ugly parts for ourselves.

We can go and answer the question: Could the equivalent of the degrees and PhDs Marion fostered for our people in those schools be found elsewhere too, like in our family's successful farmers, shopkeepers, moonshine barons, tailors, taxicab owners, salesmen, or even a generation of superstar musicians? In a place that pushed our bloodline toward success, could that be counted in Grammys and Oscars, deeds and titles to multiple farm acres, job creation from successful protesting, and other not-so-academic-looking achievements?

You can walk away from your past, and sometimes you never return, but regardless, you carry vital patches of it with you. Sometimes they are pretty, colorful pieces, and you live a peaceful life by the beauty, like my cousin Linda got to. Other times it just hurts to look at some of it. Either way, if you or your family have faced racism and yet still see more generations born in the face of it, you'll know your blood has survived it all. Each new bloodline that is formed is redrawing the picture.

Before I go, remember you can never fully close your book as long as your past still breathes somewhere unexamined and is not laid to rest. Love you or run from you (like we did my grandmother Hester), your face will still stare out from a family portrait one day, maybe with your own great- grandkids asking, "Who?" and more importantly, "Why?"

My little sister Chiquita would say to me that is the most important part— finding any and all traces of family love from all sides of each family tree. So that whatever can be remembered can grow, even through the hardness. These tough new kids must know they have roots that reach far back into the real backstory of this country. Mine is like many of theirs —a true saga of American achievement by its most oppressed and marginalized citizens. I found my personal history and encourage every one of you to find and examine your own, and by it learn more about yourselves. That's what I can leave with you as you explore your destiny.

My cousin Oscar's words are such a template for all our family sagas. He told me this:

"And I'm going to say that I believe there is a connection there somehow in my nurturing there as a kid. That is in my DNA and your own DNA. We got something from that environment that was inculcated in us. It passed through from our parents, and it refuses anything other than excellence. It insists that we not just pursue goals and dreams but that we aspire out of obligation to reach beyond ourselves to help others to do the same."

Indeed. No matter how that challenge looks to our eyes now, as I said before, there is always hope....

BIBLIOGRAPHY
CITATIONS AND REFERENCES

BBC News. 2017. "American Airlines Accused of Racism After Disturbing Incidents." October 25, 2017. http://www.bbc.com/news/world-us-canada-41754457.

Britton, Ronald. 2017. "Internal Racism: A Psychoanalytic Approach to Race and Difference." *International Journal of Psychoanalysis* 98 (2): 543. April 2017. Blackwell Publishing Ltd.

Brooks, Kelton. 2017. "Reality Intrudes upon LeBron's Iconic Status." *The Hutchinson News*, June 2, 2017.

Business Insider. 2017. "LeBron James responds after his home was vandalized with a racial slur." June 1, 2017. http://www.businessinsider.com/watch-lebron-james-responds-racist-graffiti-slur-on-home-in-la-race-emmett-till-nba-finals-2017-6.

CNN. 2017. "Another Noose Found Near DC Museum, Police Say." June 18, 2017. http://www.cnn.com/2017/06/18/us/noose-found-national-gallery-of- art/index.html

Crownover, Danny K. 1983. "Black Creek." Local history collection.
Gadsden Public Library. Cited in Jones-1989.

Fisk University History. n.d. Accessed July 2-December 5, 2017. https://www.fisk.edu/about/history.

Gadsden Times (verse). 1869. "Black Creek Falls." February 12, 1869. Quoted in part in Jones-1989.

Gaillard, Frye, Jennifer Lindsay, and Jane DeNeefe. 2010.

Alabama's Civil Rights Trail: An Illustrated Guide to the Cradle of Freedom. University of Alabama Press.

Gillespie, Marcia Ann, Rosa Johnson Butler, and Richard A. Long. 2008. Maya Angelou quote from *A Glorious Celebration.* Brilliance Audio.

Golden, Marc. 2014. "Noccalula Statue Model Dies." *Gadsden Times.* Last modified January 10, 2014. http://www.gadsdentimes.com/news/20140110/noccalula-statue-model-dies.

MENA Report. 2017. "United Kingdom: Next Steps on Tackling Hate Crime."June 2017. Albawaba (London) Ltd.

New York Times. 2014. "New York City Settles Lawsuit Accusing Fire Dept. of Racial Bias." March 19, 2014, A17.

Washington Post. 2017. "Recounting a Day of Rage, Hate, Violence and Death." http://www.washingtonpost.com/graphics/2017/local/charlottesville-timeline/?utm_term=.e2deeb3c5ba6.

Additional photos featured and sources:

Gordon Parks, photographer. 1947. "Dr. Kenneth Clark conducting the 'Doll Test' with a young male child." Gelatin silver print. Prints and Photographs Division, Library of Congress (62).

Transcribed interviews specifically for this book from Robert Avery,
Chiquita Knowles-Ash, Barbara Carstarphen-Bush, and Oscar Underwood, Jr.

US Federal Government photo. Public domain. 1963. "A Girl attending the March on Washington." August 28, 1963.

ACKNOWLEDGMENTS

First, let me give abiding gratitude to my great-parents and my fore-parents whose lives I got to know more about in the researching of this book. Without their hard-won efforts, I wouldn't even be writing these words today.

Deep appreciation to my friends and especially my family who contributed their time, recollections, and photos for the book. Many thanks to GM Garel for creative support throughout the project as well as to my graphics team for theirs.

A heartfelt thank you to my legal, accounting, administrative, and PR staff for their valuable contributions to me and Music World Entertainment. Finally, special love and gratitude to my wife Gena Avery-Knowles for her critical participation, reviews, and encouragement in pulling it all together.

ABOUT THE AUTHOR

Author, professor, lecturer, public speaker, entrepreneur, music executive, artist manager, fighter, and survivor would be the words used to sum up the life and career of Mathew Knowles, MBA, Ph.D. Knowles is widely recognized in the entertainment industry for his effective approach in developing and promoting award-winning artists.

As the founder of Music World Entertainment Corporation, he has served as the executive producer for more than 100 award-wining platinum and gold albums in multiple genres, including Pop, R&B, Gospel, Dance, Country, as well as soundtracks and special themed projects. Record sales have exceeded 450 million worldwide with work featuring some of the biggest names in music including Chaka Khan and Earth, Wind & Fire.

In Academia, Dr. Knowles has an undergraduate degree in Business Administration/Economics from Fisk University as well as Advanced Studies in Professional Development at Harvard University. He has an MBA in Strategic Planning and Organizational Culture and a Ph.D. in Business Administration from Cornerstone Christian Bible College and has held professorships at Texas Southern University, Prairie View A&M, Art Institute International, and University of Houston.

For more information, go to **Mathewknowles.com**

Lightning Source UK Ltd.
Milton Keynes UK
UKHW010037280721
387881UK00007B/423/J